Crafting the
Teachers Need and Deserve

Crafting the Feedback Teachers Need and Deserve illuminates an often overlooked aspect of educational leadership: providing quality written feedback. This resource offers context, purpose, and techniques on how to capture and write beneficial feedback. Proven in school districts, Van Soelen's strategies will accelerate improvement in classroom practice and result in teachers who crave feedback and use it to supervise themselves. Full of examples and complete with an assessment tool to gauge current practice, this book shares insights into providing effective observation and feedback within any teacher evaluation system.

Thomas M. Van Soelen is the president of Van Soelen & Associates. As a former school district leader, he now provides professional development services to schools, focusing on four areas of expertise: instructional strategies, the School Reform Initiative (SRI) Critical Friendship, leadership development, and teacher evaluation.

Other Eye On Education Books Available from Routledge (www.routledge.com/eyeoneducation)

The Leader's Guide to Working with Underperforming Teachers: Overcoming Marginal Teaching and Getting Results
Sally Zepeda

Five Critical Leadership Practices: The Secret to High-Performing Schools
Ruth C. Ash and Pat H. Hodge

Mentoring is a Verb: Strategies for Improving College and Career Readiness
Russ Olwell

How to Make Data Work: A Guide for Educational Leaders
Jenny Grant Rankin

Hiring the Best Staff for Your School: How to Use Narrative to Improve Your Recruiting Process
Rick Jetter

What Connected Educators Do Differently
Todd Whitaker, Jeffrey Zoul, and Jimmy Casas

BRAVO Principal! Building Relationships with Actions that Value Others, 2nd Edition
Sandra Harris

Job-Embedded Professional Development: Support, Collaboration, and Learning in Schools
Sally J. Zepeda

Get Organized! Time Management for School Leaders, 2nd Edition
Frank Buck

The Educator's Guide to Writing a Book: Practical Advice for Teachers and Leaders
Cathie E. West

Crafting the Feedback Teachers Need and Deserve

A Guide for Leaders

Thomas M. Van Soelen

Routledge
Taylor & Francis Group

NEW YORK AND LONDON

First published 2016
by Routledge
711 Third Avenue, New York, NY 10017

and by Routledge
2 Park Square, Milton Park, Abingdon, Oxon, OX14 4RN

Routledge is an imprint of the Taylor & Francis Group, an informa business

© 2016 Taylor & Francis

Library of Congress Cataloging-in-Publication Data
Names: Van Soelen, Thomas M., author.
Title: Crafting the feedback teachers need and deserve : a guide
    for leaders / by Thomas M. Van Soelen.
Description: New York, NY : Routledge, 2016. | Includes bibliographical references.
Identifiers: LCCN 2015038607 | ISBN 9781138949997 (hardback) |
    ISBN 9781138950030 (pbk.) | ISBN 9781315668864 (ebook)
Subjects: LCSH: Teachers—Rating of. | Teaching—Evaluation. | School supervision.
Classification: LCC LB2838 .V29 2016 | DDC 371.14/4—dc23
LC record available at http://lccn.loc.gov/2015038607

ISBN: 978-1-138-94999-7 (hbk)
ISBN: 978-1-138-95003-0 (pbk)
ISBN: 978-1-315-66886-4 (ebk)

Typeset in Optima
by Apex CoVantage, LLC

Contents

Preface   vii

Acknowledgements   xiii

Meet the Author   xv

1   **Shining the Light in the Dark**   1

2   **Why We Should Measure Feedback Quality**   21

3   **Building Your Descriptive Prowess**   37

4   **Using Conditional Language to Ponder Change**   71

5   **Why Point of View Is Significant**   93

6   **Explicitly Owning and Raising Assumptions**   117

7   **The Trickiness of Co-Teaching Situations**   145

8   **Nurturing a Culture of Feedback**   171

Appendix   193

Preface

Teaching is driving in a NASCAR race.

This intriguing metaphor needs some explanation, particularly for readers who need some background information:

In decades past, as NASCAR embraced more safety measures, full-face helmets and head-and-neck-restraint devices were required. These safety precautions significantly diminish the vision of the driver, thus causing the driver to need help from others when making weighty decisions at high rates of speed.

NASCAR drivers employ spotters. These individuals, often former drivers, sit in the stands watching the race. Their voices are electronically linked to the driver's helmets, providing a necessary perspective on the entire racetrack.

So, let's begin to apply the metaphor: teachers are driving their classrooms, feeling restrained by factors such as class size, new curriculum standards, Response to Intervention (RtI), revised teacher evaluation systems, and accountability, among others.

Back to NASCAR—the spotter doesn't simply command the driver with quips like, "Pass now!" or "Take him on this curve." Instead, the spotter stays true to the function: providing another set of eyes and ears to accommodate for the constraints. "He watches the 'blind spots'" (Boyce, 2008). The spotter's words might sound like this: "Two car lengths are now available to the right." Or "This was #23's slowest lap yet."

So a teacher has the opportunity to have a spotter in her room whenever a school leader walks in for a classroom observation. Another adult is spending time (in fact, being paid for their time) assuming this presence will matter in someone else's life—the teacher's life and the life of each student in the room. Unfortunately, that experience often does not feel helpful or even vital like a spotter is to a NASCAR driver. The spotter and the driver have a shared urgency and importance to their interactions. Often school leaders and teachers share an outcome for classroom observations, albeit unfortunate: a check mark in a "completed" column.

Like most uses of figurative language, the metaphor eventually breaks down. Teachers do not have earpieces, receiving real-time data about their classrooms like NASCAR drivers receive about their fast-paced environments. However, we would be remiss if we let the metaphor rest without the most important learning: the power of perspective.

Spotters are not on the racetrack. They are not in another car. Their position is important, germane to their job. Without their perspective, the drivers cannot be effective. Heifetz and Linsky (2002) posit this phenomenon as an analogy between being on the dance floor and standing on the balcony. Their contextual example includes dancers at a wedding. These wedding-goers may be on the dance floor thinking the band is fantastic, but those on the balcony notice that no one is dancing near the band—they are dancing as far as away as possible. The perspective from above helps others understand that although the band's execution of the notes, rhythm, and lyrics may be pleasing, the volume may be excessive.

In both metaphors, complicated work benefits from feedback and that feedback isn't primarily advice-giving. Instead, reporting what is seen and heard is highly beneficial.

Decisions

Although drivers implicitly trust their spotters to execute their job well, the driver makes the decisions, not the spotter. Similarly, rock bands have a manager who reads the crowd and offers observational feedback that might be missed in the middle of a guitar lick, drum solo, or moment of intricate harmony. However, in the middle of a concert, the manager is often powerless—the musicians make the decisions.

Educational leaders, often adorned with the unbecoming label of "administrators," often have not been trained in how to write—or better yet, craft—high-quality feedback for teaching staff. Leadership certification programs contain courses addressing mandatory content, such as educational law, special education, facilities, finance, instruction, and human resources. A fortunate graduate student could enroll in a "Supervision of Instruction" class, but even then, class activities often gravitate toward evaluation *processes* (e.g., how many observations, which observations have mandatory pre-conferences, how many days to send written feedback) and might address individual conferencing skills. How to construct written feedback to (or better yet—*for*) teachers is not addressed. I believe this is not a conscious decision by instructors; rather, the field has not identified success criteria (Wiliam, 2011) for what makes high-quality written feedback.

Audience

A young writer sits at home trying to begin her essay. She is trying out various leads:

- "I'm going to tell you about . . ." *No, that is too obvious.*
- "Most people believe . . ." *That might not even be true. I don't have an index card to support it.*
- "*The Huffington Post* reports that . . ." *How boring!*

If a teacher was providing support to this writer, a question might provoke the thinking needed to move forward: *"Who is your audience? How might they want to first hear what you are writing about?"*

Being clear about audience is critical in teaching writing. If we asked principals who was the audience of their writing for teacher evaluations, I suspect we would hear something like the following: "Audience? This isn't writing—I'm providing feedback."

We find an assistant principal on the way back to his office after a few classroom observations. "What are you going to do now?" we ask. He might say something like the following:

"I'm going to go type some feedback."
"I'm going to go knock out some feedback."
[in the southern United States, perhaps with a regional drawl] "I'm going to go get 'er done."

The audience for this book is anyone who observes classrooms and puts their thoughts down in writing. That is a much broader group than it was 20 years ago, now including principals, assistant principals, instructional coaches, central office instructional leaders, department chairs, teacher mentors, university practicum supervisors, and colleagues engaging in peer observation.

Using the principles found in this book, feedback will be *crafted*. Language matters and the word choices we make have direct impact on the willingness of the readers, the teachers, to consider the observation as a meaningful input for accelerating improvements in classroom practice.

Crafting something requires skill, diligence, and study. Certainly knowing the skills of effective instruction, respectful classroom management, and rigorous assessment will assist in the content requirements of understanding classrooms; however, that is not enough. We must write feedback that teachers crave.

Start Your Engines

Perhaps as a leader you need a spotter, like the NASCAR driver. Before showing your feedback to others, it might make sense to take time and learn what high-quality feedback looks like and sounds like. Just like a budding pianist or an emerging tennis player, small bursts of practice combined with clear feedback create a promising learning cycle.

I doubt there is a contingent of leaders that intentionally provide sub-standard feedback. It is more probable that we lack the criteria for what makes useful feedback. Once we know those descriptors, we can then choose whether to work toward them.

Measuring feedback quality is not a popular topic in educational literature, but the intersection of several lines of inquiry pose this exploration as worthwhile. Chapter 2 briefly explores each line and their connections.

Chapter 3 begins the identification of the skills necessary to write high-quality feedback and positions us to give ourselves feedback on our feedback! This book builds a compelling case for each of the desired outcomes (skills) found in the High-Quality Feedback Innovation Configuration Map, one chapter at a time starting with Chapter 3. The chapters contain numerous examples and non-examples from a variety of schools and school settings.

At the end of each of chapter, small experiences called "Try It Yourself" are included that can be attempted individually or with colleagues. These activities are primarily harvested from my direct experiences with school leaders. A consistent feature in these closing segments are these questions: What practices from this chapter are 10-degree changes? Which might require a 90-degree change in your practice? I use this 10/90 structure often in professional development for educators to first document their learning and then prioritize it.

Also present in some "Try It Yourself" sections is a connection to protocols, like the *ATLAS Looking at Data* protocol described in Chapter 1. The strong research base that has informed and popularized the use of protocols ("structured conversations") has a clear influence on this book and the High-Quality Feedback Innovation Configuration Map. Several dispositions and ways of looking have been applied to teacher evaluation.

The book closes with Chapter 8, which details the shifts that leaders may experience as they develop these skills, and explains how to prepare teachers to accept and use written feedback that looks and sounds different. Oral feedback is not the subject of this book. Neither is how to have face-to-face coaching conversations. Many other writers (Jim Knight, Art Costa) offer clear success criteria for those conversations. However, with the increased frequency of classroom observations in many teacher evaluation systems, it is incumbent on school leaders to craft written feedback that is productive and helpful with *or* without a face-to-face conference.

Reference List

Boyce, T.V. (December 5, 2008). *How does a NASCAR driver communicate with the pit crew?* Retrieved from http://auto.howstuffworks.com/auto-racing/nascar/jobs/nascar-driver-communicate.htm.

Heifetz, R.A., & Linsky, M. (2002). *Leadership on the line: Staying alive through the dangers of leading.* Boston, MA: Harvard Business.

Wiliam, D. (2011). *Embedded formative assessment.* Bloomington, IN: Solution Tree.

Acknowledgements

Writing a book wasn't part of *the* plan or any plan. It almost became a necessity in helping other schools and districts understand the impact that high-quality feedback has on the readers of that feedback, the teachers. As I provided more large-group professional development, engaged in more co-observations, and analyzed more video clips, this volume started to take shape. The best part of instructional leadership is present here: diligently working to give adults feedback on their core work.

I extend thanks to clients who gave of their time, energy, and most importantly, their products as they grew in their proficiency. I am so appreciative to the school principals in the Brookwood cluster in Lawrenceville, GA (Tonya Burnley, Cheri Carter, Bo Ford, Peggy Goodman, Karen Head, Christine Knox, Stacey Schepens, and Angie Wright), as well as Chuck Bell, superintendent of Elbert County Schools, GA. Other GA leaders have been part of this product development as we have co-observed and learned with and from each other (Jennifer Adams, Billy Heaton, Dion Jones, Laura Mason, Susan Stanton, and Evelyn Wages).

I am thankful to members of a monthly learning community engaged in the School Reform Initiative critical friendship who gathered to offer feedback on an early chapter draft. These folks made a difference in the content and organization of the volume: Donna Ledford, Dan McGuire, Daniel Skelton, and Marci Sledge. Marci and Mike Nekritz from Chicago also provided specific feedback to Routledge—thank you.

The leadership at Alpharetta High School deserves a significant note here, as they have embraced the desired outcomes described in this book. Principal Shannon Kersey, her assistant principals, and her department chairs take feedback-writing seriously and consider it one of the most important things they do as leaders.

Without City Schools of Decatur, GA, this wouldn't have happened. Raising teacher quality became our bailiwick as we ventured into uncharted territory. I am so proud of the work we accomplished together and joyful that Routledge saw fit to put our story into print.

A family of educators, perhaps unknowingly, brought me to this juncture, and for that I am quite delighted. I offer gratitude to Tim, Jill, Kim, and my parents, Jan and Marion—all educators.

My path into collaborative leadership was greatly shaped by divinely scheduled collaborations with Betty Bisplinghoff, Frances Hensley, and Connie Zimmerman Parrish. These three teacher-educators and school reformers introduced me to (and nourished me in) the processes and protocols of the School Reform Initiative critical friendship. I am forever grateful for their continued shaping of my interactions with adults.

Finally, to my family: children Addison and Sullivan, sources of endless delight and frustration, I am so pleased to have this finished. They gave me space and encouragement along the way. Whenever Sullivan, a five-year-old, offered unsolicited feedback on my driving, food choices, or lawn mowing technique, Julie, my wife, reminded me: "You can't be frustrated at him—you are writing a book about feedback, after all."

I give thanks to Julie, one of the best teachers I know, for her eternal patience and, more importantly, the courage to keep me grounded in the everyday work of teachers and students in classrooms.

Meet the Author

Dr. Thomas M. Van Soelen enjoys creating and participating in collaborative experiences everywhere he goes. Currently, as the president of Van Soelen & Associates, a professional development and leadership coaching consulting firm based in Lawrenceville, Georgia, Thomas influences schools and school districts that are ethnically, linguistically, and socioeconomically diverse. His client list includes organizations in Georgia (e.g., Gwinnett County Public Schools, Fulton County Schools, Georgia State Superintendent Association), Texas (e.g., Lewisville Independent School District (ISD), Garland ISD, Arlington ISD, Fort Worth ISD, Learning Forward Texas), and in Canada and Guyana.

His primary areas of expertise include teacher evaluation, instructional coaching, leadership development, and learning communities. In particular, Thomas prepares district, school, and teacher leaders to organize effective and efficient collaborative sessions, focused on student learning using structured conversations called protocols, promulgated through the School Reform Initiative.

Prior to this entrepreneurial venture, Thomas worked in multiple states and in public and private schools, teaching every grade level from prekindergarten through graduate school at some point in his career. His most recent school district leadership position was functioning as the associate superintendent in the City Schools of Decatur, Georgia, a post he held for eight years. During that time, he began a gathering of principals engaged in critical friendship through the School Reform Initiative. This voluntary group first met in 2010 and still regularly meets to learn with and from each other.

Thomas, his wife, and their two sons live near Atlanta, where Thomas now enters his third decade as a church musician, leading choirs and playing piano and organ.

Shining the Light in the Dark

This book stems from a five-year inquiry in the City Schools of Decatur (CSD), Georgia. CSD is a public school system in metro Atlanta ranking as one of the largest 600 school districts in the United States with approximately 4,250 learners in kindergarten through grade 12 and another 350 children in an early learning center (birth to age four). In the early 2000s, the community reported high-performing schools, but a lack of disaggregated data shielded parents and educators from a significant achievement gap—in some content areas, triple the national average.

As school reform models and instructional improvements were implemented through a widespread strategic plan, the lackluster teacher evaluation plan initially remained untouched. Although the strategic plan seemed to generate immediate spikes in achievement, the pace of student growth slowed. Focus turned to the adults, and teacher evaluation was in the crosshairs.

As the current reality was defined, it became increasingly clear that not only was the teacher evaluation process unrigorous, it was not used with fidelity. As teacher-level data was examined, very little difference emerged in the evaluation practices and results of two teachers with sizable achievement differences. Upon reading and studying, this wasn't shocking: "A review in 2008 of teacher evaluations in [Hillsborough County, Florida] found that more than 99% of the 12,000 teachers were rated as satisfactory or outstanding, and nearly half of high school teachers received perfect scores" (von Frank, 2011).

The priority was determined and time carved out. District leaders used strategies that had previously worked in other areas of school improvement:

- Reading professional texts defining terms such as learning targets and assessment
- Observing classrooms in pairs
- Working slowly, not implementing everything immediately

As the observational prowess seemed to improve, district leaders heard from faculty. "Outspoken teachers appreciated the increased feedback frequency but desired qualitative responses as well. Some even pointed to one of the teaching standards that delineated the criteria of effective written and verbal feedback for student learners, questioning our premise of explicitly modeling these standards in our own work with adults" (Van Soelen, 2013). Said in another way: "You expect us to write high-quality feedback for our students; you aren't writing high-quality feedback for us."

Inter-Rater Reliability Is Not Enough

New teacher evaluation systems often breed needs for school leaders to calibrate their evaluation ratings across observers. Sometimes this work happens in individual schools, other times across a school district. These sorts of healthy debates and shared focus can prove positive: inter-rater reliability can grow. Unique models like cross-school teacher evaluation can greatly accelerate this outcome (Van Soelen, 2012).

However, growing in alignment did not meet teachers' articulated need for high-quality feedback—it simply meant that Decatur teachers were experiencing evaluations that were more consistent across the district.

It is *that* inquiry which was developed into an assessment tool, and eventually, this book. By this point, the Decatur professional development group had grown, now including at least one teacher leader from each school. These outstanding teachers helped the group see that the rubric ratings (1–4) had limited impact: they might spur a teacher to more thoroughly read the rubric, but without written narrative feedback, teachers are left to wonder what evidence really informed the rating.

It was risky to have such an integrated group of teachers and leaders, but it paid great dividends. An even larger risk was looming as the first video clip was queued up: we were going to show each other our written feedback.

Using electronic tools, such as PollEverywhere.com and Google Forms, leaders wrote feedback and clicked "submit" for all to see.

A Spotlight

A principal described the experience best: "A spotlight has just been shined in a dark corner." Remember the course sequence of leadership preparation programs? Even 20 years of being a principal doesn't necessarily improve your written feedback. A similarly faulty analogy would be that your swimming strokes will improve by simply standing in water more frequently.

Although increasing quantity does not necessarily equate with improved aptitude, risk can become less risky the more often you engage in it or with it. And so it happened with sharing our feedback. The anonymity of the web-based tools assisted with the risk-taking, as did strategic partnering both during professional development sessions and during shared classroom observations in the cross-school teacher evaluation processes. More detail on Decatur's story is available (Van Soelen, 2013).

After repeated failed attempts to create a high-quality feedback rubric, one group searched for another tool that would meet their outcomes. They stumbled upon an Innovation Configuration Map.

> An Innovation Configuration Map (Hord, et al., 2006) was chosen to codify what we defined as high-quality feedback because Innovation Configurations elucidate concepts and make seemingly invisible practices explicit while also setting expectations within an array of variations. Innovation Configurations emerged from the Concerns-Based Adoption Model (Hord, et al., 1987), describing an innovation in action while the Innovation Configuration Map clarifies what the innovation looks like across a continuum of practice.
>
> (Van Soelen, 2013, p. 28)

The finished product is represented as Table 1.1. Each row lists a desired outcome in the first column with a corresponding purpose. The first draft

Table 1.1 High-Quality Feedback Innovation Configuration Map

Description	1	2	3	4
Purpose: to see and hear what's going on in a classroom	Feedback is highly **descriptive**, balancing rich descriptions of student behaviors and teacher behaviors. Feedback includes **data** that was seen and heard, using direct **quotations** when appropriate. *"Three students put their heads down during the 10-minute movie, near the 6-minute mark. You remained at the back of the room speaking once to a student. It appeared that 10 students wrote something down. One student near the door used a Flow Map."*	Feedback is mostly **descriptive**, including **approximations** for what was seen and/or heard. Feedback may include student behaviors as well as teacher behaviors. *"Three students slept during the 10-minute movie. You remained at the back of the room watching the movie with the students."*	Feedback uses primarily **evaluative** and **interpretive** language. Feedback may include student behaviors as well as teacher behaviors. *"Students appeared off-task and bored during the movie despite your directions for them to take notes."*	Feedback primarily draws on **evaluative** language. Feedback is limited to teacher behaviors. *"You allowed the sleeping students too long before you intervened."*

Conditional Language *Purpose:* to ponder a possible gap in practice	Conditional language is effectively used to help the reader **deeply consider gaps** or unintended results. *"At least three standards in this observation appear to be affected by students' responsibilities when they arrive to class."*	Conditional language is effectively used that would spur the reader to **pause and consider.** *"It seems that there may be a connection between instructional time lost and classroom routines."*	Conditional language is used to offer **suggestions.** *"We are curious about the potential if students had a consistent routine every time they entered their room."*	**Rhetorical questions** are used to suggest. *"What might happen if you had something up on the ACTIVBoard the first moment students entered the room?"*
Point of View *Purpose:* to accept the feedback more about practice than the person	Feedback primarily focuses on **actions** instead of the teacher. Passive voice pervades the feedback. *"The ACTIVBoard was used to model the Circle Map."*	Feedback is primarily written focusing on the **observer.** *"I observed that the ACTIVBoard was used to model the Circle Map."*	Feedback is primarily written from **another person's** point of view. *"**You** used the ACTIVBoard to model the Circle Map."* *"**The teacher** used the ACTIVBoard to model the Circle Map."* *"**Ms. Smith** used the ACTIVBoard to model the Circle Map."*	

(Continued)

Table 1.1 (Continued)

	1	2	3	4
Assumptions *Purpose:* to acknowledge the observer has a partial picture	Assumptions inherent in the feedback are **explicitly** identified. *"Students identified that group composition sometimes changes. The grouping rationale was difficult to ascertain today."*	Assumptions are drawn from observational evidence. The assumptions are **not recognized** or identified by the observer. *"Flexible groups are used to offer students more opportunities to learn with others."*	Assumptions are drawn from the **lack of observational evidence.** The assumptions are not recognized or identified by the observer. *"Consider having the groups organized in more intentional ways based on assessment."*	
Co-Teaching Model *Purpose:* to identify purposes and jobs of multiple adults in classrooms	In co-teaching situations, the identified co-teaching model(s) serves as a **foundation** for the feedback. *"The Tree Map drawn on the board by Ms. Smith as complementary co-teaching while you were discussing was referenced three times by students later in the discussion."*	In co-teaching situations, feedback is **related** to the co-teaching model(s) used but the model is not identified. *"Ms. Smith drew a Tree Map on the whiteboard as you discussed with students."*	In co-teaching situations, the co-teaching model(s) is identified but **disconnected** from any feedback. *"Today's lesson used the Complementary Co-Teaching model."*	In co-teaching situations, **nothing** in the feedback **reflects on the reality** of multiple adults present in the classroom. *[Feedback does not reference multiple adults in the classroom.]*

	1	2	3	4
Co-Teaching Equity *Purpose:* to not reinforce hierarchies between adults	In co-teaching situations, language focuses on **equity:** on the **action** rather than the person. *"One Teach, One Observe was used. This content seems to need a co-teaching model where both adults are more actively engaged with students."*	In co-teaching situations, language suggests **power:** "having" another colleague do something. *"Consider having your co-teacher alternatively teach during your mini-lesson."*		

included the first four desired outcomes, emerging from the group's professional development sessions and teacher feedback. As the group continued to learn together, analysis of written feedback and leader reflections identified writing feedback in co-teaching situations as the growing edge for this group. After exploring the content of co-teaching and then writing feedback in co-teaching situations, the last two desired outcomes were crafted.

Level 1 represents the ideal, and any variations are described in cells to the right of the ideal. Notice the six desired outcomes have differing numbers of variations, ranging from 2 to 4. The number of variations was determined by the group as they examined the submitted feedback from their colleagues. The gray shading on this Innovation Configuration Map remains as an example of how expectations are set, as each gray cell represents an unacceptable variation. You might set expectations differently and choose to apply grayscale to different cells.

The next professional development session provided the perfect context to test-drive the new Innovation Configuration Map. A fresh video clip of a tough-to-assess teaching element played, partners attempted to write feedback using the Innovation Configuration Map, and, as was our practice, wrote reflections before they exited:

The innovation configuration is making me rethink what all of our assumptions are in regards to feedback.

(principal)

The idea of having this tool to help with improving my feedback is comforting yet makes me wonder if I have fallen short with some of my recent feedback—a good wondering.

(assistant principal)

This is hard.

(principal)

Today's learning was helpful because it helped me work on really quality feedback. Really concentrating on third person, what you see and hear. . . . It also helps me understand better the feedback that I get.

(teacher)

The format and intensity of the professional development sessions provided natural accountability for the leaders, but some wanted more. The week following the learning using the Innovation Configuration Map, two principals each requested a visit from a district office instructional leader to work with them on their feedback.

Getting Feedback on Our Feedback

It may seem paradoxical to posit that written feedback about classroom practice is a dark place for leaders. It's clearly on paper. It's clearly presented to someone else. What makes it dark—out of the light?

For decades, because of supervisory dynamics and irrelevant teacher evaluation systems, it was quite uncommon for teachers to offer dissenting opinions about written feedback. It was simply easier for teachers to stay quiet and wait it out. Tenure and/or unions often protected them from taking the feedback too seriously.

Teachers in a middle school hallway I know use code words with each other when the administrators are out and about, observing for the annual evaluations. A mathematics teacher may be in the hallway between classes and state to the teacher in the next classroom: "Just letting you know—my feet are up and I'm smokin'." Although neither are true—feet up nor smoking in a classroom—the language indicates she was just observed and she is now done. This response also shows there is very little expectation the feedback will matter for her professional growth.

So school leaders are not frequently receiving feedback on *their* written feedback from teaching staff. Are they receiving feedback from anybody else?

I recently supported a leadership team who was implementing a new teacher evaluation system. Although the team had calibrated the 1–4 rating scale multiple times, they acknowledged that the quality of written feedback probably varied between the principal and the four assistants.

"I've been a principal for 15 years and I don't think anyone but the teacher has read a one of these." The principal decided to make his private practices a bit more public, so using written feedback from a formative observation, he showed his assistant principals his written narrative. Although the principal made it clear that he "could handle it" and that the assistants should "say what [they] really think," a structured conversation, a protocol, provided both the necessary parameters and the space to muster up courage. We chose to treat the written feedback as a data set, using *ATLAS Looking at Data* (Leahy, n.d.) as our conversation structure.

ATLAS Looking at Data

1. Getting Started
   a. The facilitator reminds the group of the norms.
   b. The educator providing the data set gives a very brief statement of the data and avoids explaining what she/he concludes about the data if the data belongs to the group rather than the presenter.
   c. Note: Each of the next 4 steps should be about 10 minutes in length. It is sometimes helpful for the facilitator to take notes.

2. Describing the Data
   a. The facilitator asks: "What do you see?"
   b. During this period the group gathers as much information as possible from the data.
   c. Group members describe what they see in data, avoiding judgments about quality or interpretations. It is helpful to identify where the observation is being made—e.g., "On page one in the second column, third row . . ."
   d. If judgments or interpretations do arise, the facilitator should ask the person to describe the evidence on which they are based.
   e. It may be useful to list the group's observations on chart paper. If interpretations come up, they can be listed in another column for later discussion during Step 3.

3. Interpretating the Data
   a. The facilitator asks: "What does the data suggest?" Followed by—"What are the assumptions we make about students and their learning?"

b. During this period, the group tries to make sense of what the data says and why. The group should try to find as many different interpretations as possible and evaluate them against the kind and quality of evidence.

c. From the evidence gathered in the preceding section, try to infer: What is being worked on and why?

d. Think broadly and creatively. Assume that the data, no matter how confusing, makes sense to some people; your job is to see what they may see.

e. As you listen to each other's interpretations, ask questions that help you better understand each other's perspectives.

4. Implications for Classroom Practice

a. The facilitator asks: "What are the implications of this work for teaching and assessment?" This question may be modified, depending on the data.

b. Based on the group's observations and interpretations, discuss any implications this work might have for teaching and assessment in the classroom. In particular, consider the following questions:

  i. What steps could be taken next?

  ii. What strategies might be most effective?

  iii. What else would you like to see happen? What kinds of assignments or assessments could provide this information?

  iv. What does this conversation make you think about in terms of your own practice? About teaching and learning in general?

  v. What are the implications for equity?

5. Reflecting on the ATLAS Looking at Data

a. Presenter Reflection:

  i. What did you learn from listening to your colleagues that was interesting or surprising?

  ii. What new perspectives did your colleagues provide?

  iii. How can you make use of your colleagues' perspectives?

b. Group Reflection:

    i. What questions about teaching and assessment did looking at the data raise for you?

    ii. Did questions of equity arise?

    iii. How can you pursue these questions further?

    iv. Are there things you would like to try in your classroom as a result of looking at this data?

6. Debrief the Process

    a. How well did the process work?

    b. What about the process helped you to see and learn interesting or surprising things?

    c. What could be improved?

Reprinted with permission of Dianne Leahy.

The principal took notes for steps 1–4, staying quiet (mostly) for almost 30 minutes as the group described, interpreted, and drew implications for their work in crafting feedback. His return to the conversation offered several changes in his practice that he wanted to make (e.g., provide more evidence, think carefully how often to give advice, use a consistent point of view), but more importantly, he noted: "I underestimated how hard it would be to sit here, listening to feedback. I give it all the time but rarely put myself in a position to ask for it. Don't get me wrong—it was so helpful. But it was so hard."

The same protocol was used in a group of principals who voluntarily meet using the principles and practices of School Reform Initiative critical friendship. A middle school principal brought an observation write-up and listened in as her principal colleagues from nearby schools richly mined her words, wondered about their meaning, and admitted their own shortcomings in crafting the feedback that teachers need and deserve.

Principal supervisors or the human resources department would seem like logical sources of feedback on a task that represents a significant commitment of principals' time. Readers of this book might attest to the dearth of central office leaders providing principals with meaningful feedback about teacher evaluation practices other than when school leaders sometimes miss evaluation deadlines.

Formatively Speaking

So you might be crafting some high-quality feedback and you didn't even know it. Right now you lack the data *to make decisions:* to repeat what works and discard what doesn't.

In this way, classroom observation has a strong connection to formative assessment. Formative assessment is a highly misunderstood practice. Similar to workshops offered by formative assessment experts (Wiliam, 2011; Arter & Chappuis, 2013; Stiggins, 2014), my professional development about formative assessment often begins by combatting misconceptions. Here are a few responses I've received when facilitating around this topic:

- "It's formative because it's a quiz."
- "I entered it in the formative category in my gradebook."
- "We're in the middle of the unit, therefore it's formative."
- "Well, it isn't summative, so it must be formative."
- "Look—it says it right here in the title—'formative.'"

I subscribe to a shortened version of Wiliam's (2011) definition for formative assessment. Three tests exist if something is acting in a formative way:

1. Was something collected?
2. Was it clear for what purpose and for whom it would be collected?
3. What decision(s) was made because of the collection?

Or an even shorter version:

1. Collect something.
2. Know for whom and why it was collected.
3. Make a decision.

It often helps educators by challenging them to remove "assessment" from the term, at least temporarily, if needed. What makes something *formative?*

Then instead of asking, "Was that ticket out the door a formative assessment?" we would ask, "In what ways was that ticket out the door used formatively, and if so, by whom for what purpose?"

Observers often assume the byproduct of classroom observations is #3 above: "make a decision" or more directly, "make some changes." An assistant principal shared with me recently that she had collected six 30-minute observations on Friday. "I'm behind," she lamented, as she drew close to a district deadline. Her Saturday was not spent with her young children, or preparing for an upcoming parent meeting regarding special education goals, or submitting a conference proposal for the district summer learning conference. You guessed it—she spent five hours on Saturday writing these observations. This young woman is determined that the recipients of her labor, these teachers, will engage in #3, upon reading her carefully worded responses.

Hours spent in distinguishing the "just right" language does not necessarily equate to meaningful feedback. I have discovered the opposite. This is not to say that thoughtful choices about language don't matter! I am experiencing that very necessity as I ponder what words to use in delivering the thoughts in this book. Instead, leaders default to summarizing rather than letting the description provide an opportunity for the recipient, the teacher, to truly think. Most summaries don't provoke the reader to make a decision, thus they do not meet test #3 above, and therefore the narratives are not used formatively.

Consider this observation sent to a teacher:

> *The discussion with students was rich! Everyone was engaged and really enjoyed the discussion.*
> *It is obvious that Mrs. Kilpatrick has developed a positive rapport with her students and created a classroom where students want to come. It is also evident that clear classroom rules and procedures have been established.*

A colleague of mine is a 20-year teaching veteran and still becomes markedly nervous around observation times. Her school engages in the bare minimum and usually notifies teachers that the observation rounds have begun. If they don't send anything out publicly, emails and texts between teachers communicate the message quite expediently. She has a doctoral degree, multiple endorsements and certifications, and a publication—but those don't matter, as her nerves spike when someone is in the back of her room typing away.

The feedback listed two paragraphs prior was posted to her teacher evaluation portal just in the nick of time to meet the five-day response window. It begs a few questions:

1. What made the discussion "rich"?
2. Every kid was "engaged"? Every kid "enjoyed" it? How did the observer know?
3. What does "positive rapport" look like and sound like in this classroom?
4. Why did it take five whole days to write *this* up?

And, finally,

5. Who is Mrs. Kilpatrick?

Yes, this administrator was caught in the too-often act of copying and pasting. My colleague's name is *not* Mrs. Kilpatrick and never has been.

Although that major blunder is certainly serious enough that a teacher might disregard the entire document, a larger issue exists: Where is the evidence? Summaries inadvertently create conditions that encourage teachers to ignore, and even worse, mock classroom observation results.

I am often a bit breathless upon exiting a classroom. My senses have been on high alert and my fingers have been flying on the keyboard. More specific strategies are included in Chapter 8 about how to prepare school faculties for this feedback shift, but the amount of feedback collected is one of those very items. In current practice, if an observer is busy typing away, a teacher may think one of two things is going on:

1. This observation isn't going well, and she has tons to say.
2. She is checking email.

Or even worse, a combination of both. Katie Wagner remembers her principal's brief observation last fall:

> He entered during third period when I don't have any chairs available—a student even sits in mine. Miraculously this day

one chair was empty at a back table. So, he sat, facing *the back wall,* and opened his computer. As I was engaged in some direct instruction, I saw him respond to emails. Our email program is easily identifiable. He walked out 15 minutes later. I sweated it several days until the feedback appeared in the portal.

Here's Katie's feedback from her 15-minute "observation" of the back wall:

Instructional Strategies: Proficient
   Students worked in groups to discuss their current events. You taught strategies on how to read the text. You used their foldable to tie prior knowledge to what they were learning. You demonstrated and modeled how to use the reading strategy.

Compare this feedback to how Principal Kent Isakson reflected when he observed Wanda Xavier:

I went in for math small group and sat by the kidney table. I knew her teaching pace was often quick, so I took a breath as I opened my laptop and began. When I left 15 minutes later, I wasn't sure what to do. I had typed more than 35 questions in that timeframe.

A few samples of collected questions:

What is the largest unit, what's next, what's next, what's the smallest?
Yesterday when we made our anchor chart what operation do we use?
When we go from smallest to biggest, what operation do we use?
Multiple times: CM, what are we multiplying and dividing by?
Multiple times: KM, what are we multiplying and dividing by?
10 × 7?
Seventy what?
What are we trying to change?
Does anyone have any questions?

Kent: "I trusted my description and sent it off. The next day I received a one-sentence response from Wanda: 'Data provides motivation.' That said it. I certainly didn't need to say anything else and was quite glad I hadn't." The next time Kent observed this classroom, not only did Wanda ask fewer questions, those that were asked were of higher quality with increased rigor.

Knowing/Doing Gap

So why is this so hard? Leaders are experienced educators and know what effective feedback looks like and sounds like, right? Quite often, wrong.

Many leaders were encouraged to enter administration based on stellar teaching and stellar teachers often receive less feedback. Sometimes this is an intentional move—a principal has 60 minutes to engage in classroom observations and finds herself near your classroom door. A Jewish Passover-esque experience occurs as she consciously decides to "pass you over" and observe classrooms with more instructional or management gaps.

Unintentional feedback gaps can occur even if the observations do take place. I know a principal who has a particular classroom he goes to when he needs to either escape his office or center himself before re-entering the grind. It is logical to assume the classroom he chooses is of high-quality or his hiatus would not be enjoyed. It is also doubtful this teacher receives feedback on these classroom visits and has probably learned not to expect any. If she does receive any feedback, it probably is full of praise, and possibly requests for others to observe in her classroom.

Some principals report having been *that teacher*—the classroom where their former principal spent extra time. So, either way, a stellar teacher who received few observations or a stellar teacher who received few pieces of meaningful written feedback—these leaders are being asked to create something of which they have no models or direct experience. If leaders saw this kind of gap in classrooms with students, I bet some feedback would be written to address it!

As a math teacher from Nathan Hale High School put it, "I love when Ms. Donaldson comes to my room. She catches everything—what I'm doing, what the kids say, their reactions . . . it is so helpful. And I don't need to wait long for it, she sends it right away!"

So are you ready to craft?

Try It Yourself

1. What's your metaphor when you are in a classroom observation? "When I'm at my best as a classroom observer, I am . . ." Share these with each person in your building that engages in observation. Discuss the strengths and limitations of each metaphor. This process is fully delineated as a protocol from the School Reform Initiative: *Creating Metaphors* (http://schoolreforminitiative.org/doc/creating_metaphors.pdf).

2. In a whole group faculty meeting, ask teaching staff to create a metaphor for themselves as teachers. Then consider modifying the *Creating Metaphors* process, asking teachers to identify metaphors that leaders could consider when crafting the very best classroom feedback.

3. Consider using *ATLAS Looking at Data* (http://schoolreforminitiative.org/doc/atlas_looking_data.pdf) with other observers (either in your school or in other schools) as a way to gain fresh perspective on your own observation skills before you study and practice the skills found in this book.

4. Consider your learning from this chapter: What practices from this chapter are 10-degree changes? Which might require a 90-degree change in your practice? What might be first on your docket?

Reference List

Arter, J.A., & Chappuis, J. (2013). *Classroom assessment for student learning: Doing it right – using it well*. New York, NY: Pearson.

Hord, S., Rutherford, W., Huling-Austin, L., & Hall, G. (1987). *Taking charge of change*. Alexandria, VA: Association for Supervision and Curriculum Development.

Hord, S., Stiegelbauer, S., Hall, G., & George, A. (2006). *Measuring implementation in schools: Innovation configurations*. Austin, TX: Southwest Educational Development Laboratory.

Leahy, D. (n.d.). *ATLAS looking at data*. Retrieved from http://www.schoolreforminitiative.org/doc/atlas_looking_data.pdf.

Stiggins, R. (2014). *Revolutionize assessment: Empower students, inspire learning.* Thousand Oaks, CA: Corwin.

Van Soelen, T.M. (September, 2012). Cross-school teacher evaluation. *The New Superintendent's E-Journal,* American Association of School Administrators.

Van Soelen, T.M., (2013). Building a sustainable culture of feedback. *Performance Improvement Journal, 52*(4), 22–29.

Von Frank, V. (2011). Measurement makeover. *Journal of Staff Development, 32*(6), 32–39.

Wiliam, D. (2011). *Embedded formative assessment.* Bloomington, IN: Solution Tree.

Why We Should Measure Feedback Quality

> The potency of formative teacher evaluation—a process from which most teachers and their students benefit substantially.
>
> (Popham, 2013, p. 18)

It is unfortunate that thousands of teachers each year endure a teacher evaluation process that does not inspire or instigate any changes in their practice. The amount of human capital that is spent on the activities required in most teacher evaluation systems is staggering, yet the return on the investment is often nil.

It is a crime that schools spend energy on actions that don't have substantial impact. By the time you finish reading this paragraph, I suspect you could name 10 actions you regularly take in schools that do not have direct sightlines to student achievement. The larger atrocity is that most adults employed in schools do not think that teacher evaluation actually *can* have a meaningful impact on teacher practice and student achievement.

In working with districts and schools that wish to create high-quality feedback systems, I often use a *Continuum Dialogue* (http://schoolreform initiative.org/doc/continuum_dialogue.pdf) to start off our learning. Participants stand and place their body like a point of data on a line extending from two extremes, as in Figure 2.1.

As individuals place themselves at any point along this continuum, they are asked to provide evidence that substantiates their perception. Sometimes conversations happen in pairs, small groups, or a whole group.

Figure 2.1 focuses on the current state of a school or a district. If now framed around beliefs, the poles look like Figure 2.2.

Our teacher evaluation system is a bureaucratic system of checkboxes and deadlines.

Our teacher evaluation system is a school improvement strategy.

Figure 2.1 Continuum Dialogue Poles

I believe our teacher evaluation system will always be a bureaucratic system of checkboxes and deadlines.

I believe our teacher evaluation system could be a relevant school improvement strategy.

Figure 2.2 Continuum Dialogue Poles Re: Beliefs

I have never experienced a school where everyone was willing to stand near the right side—it is so far removed from their lived experience that they cannot even imagine a reality where that occurs. The quality of the feedback matters.

This chapter details the lines of educational research inquiry that substantiate the reality of the right side, resulting in more consciously competent educators that are ready to "autosupervise" (Zepeda et al., 1996).

Consciousness and Competence

Noel Burch, a business training expert, created the Conscious Competence Ladder in the 1970s. He sought to bring structure to the frequently messy process of organizational learning. His ladder is represented in Figure 2.3.

At first glance, the concept looks quite simple, but do not let the small prefixes fool you. Trainers in various professions have used these concepts for the past 40 years in various ways for participants to engage in the following:

- Understand their emotions during learning
- Self-motivate toward another "rung" of the ladder
- Retain the perspective of what it felt like to be in the Unconscious Incompetence stage

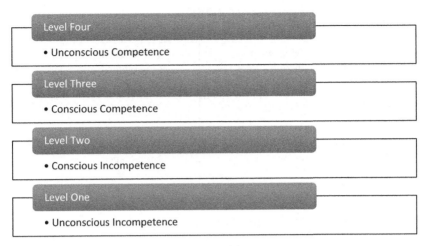

Level Four
• Unconscious Competence

Level Three
• Conscious Competence

Level Two
• Conscious Incompetence

Level One
• Unconscious Incompetence

Figure 2.3 Conscious Competence Ladder

Presenters and trainers also use the ladder to focus their own actions:

- Plan training
- Measure outputs
- Coach participants

The Conscious Competence Ladder is more frequently visualized as a 2 × 2 matrix similar to a Johari window, as demonstrated in Figure 2.4. In this model, the end goal is to be able to use the learned skills and behaviors consistently and effortlessly—demonstrating Unconscious Competence. At that stage, success is inevitable so the mind does not need to exert energy on the actions.

I was a 110-meter high hurdler in high school, and my coach clearly wanted to move me to Unconscious Competence. I started at Unconscious Incompetence with hurdles (after I was consciously incompetent at running long distances and the high jump). Since I was the tallest guy on the team, hurdles seemed like an obvious match. I wasn't in that stage for long as I learned how hard it was to keep consistent form over each hurdle. Although Mr. Bouma kindly enacted initial modifications of height and substance (i.e., replaced the 39" wood hurdles with 33" foam hurdles), I still stayed in Conscious Incompetence for some time.

As with most sports training, repeated attempts can build toward competence, and this was one of those cases. I began making my way down all

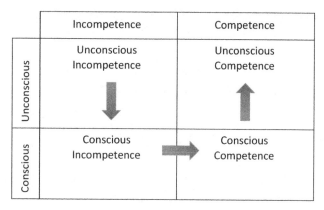

Figure 2.4 Conscious Competence Ladder as a Johari Window

10 hurdles, clearing each one with consistent form. However, in between each hurdle I was still counting "1, 2, 3" to measure my steps. It may have been my senior year when I moved into Unconscious Competence—but not until after the first hurdle. I never was able to make my starts automatic, much to the chagrin of Mr. Bouma. Applying this training matrix to my athletic stories makes sense, both in terms of the progression and the end result.

Burch and Maslow

This ladder and theory are often misattributed to psychologist Abraham Maslow. Perhaps most famous for articulating the hierarchy of needs (Figure 2.5), the fifth stage: Self-Actualization, is frequently misaligned to Unconscious Competence. Individuals who demonstrate Self-Actualization are very aware of their actions as well as the intended and unintended consequences.

"Self-actualizing people are not dependent for their main satisfactions on the real world, or other people or culture or means-to-ends, or in general, on extrinsic satisfactions. Rather they are dependent for their own development and continued growth upon their own potentialities and latent resources" (Maslow, 1973, p. 188).

Here is an example of how this works in schools: Ms. McCormick, an elementary school teacher, had been keeping most of her mathematics essential questions and learning intentions the same, despite the transition

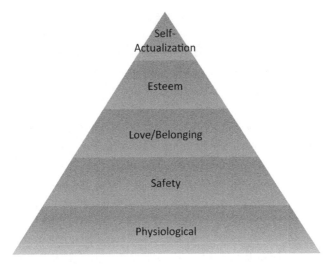

Figure 2.5 Maslow's Hierarchy of Needs

to the Common Core State Standards. Her reasoning: "The math is the same the kids need to do, so I just need to change the numbering of the standards to prove I taught them."

An observer has pointed out her learning intentions do not match the rigor of the new standards. Apparently she demonstrated Unconscious Incompetence in this area. She now must make a choice: Will she change the learning intentions or not?

Choice 1: Change Them

Ms. McCormick chooses to change the learning intentions, better matching them to the standard, thus altering the content of the guided math lessons. She has complied with the spirit of the request, but may not really know why this matters for her students. In other words, she moves to Unconscious Competence.

Choice 2: Don't Change Them

She doesn't believe yet that the learning intentions are truly misaligned, thinking this feedback is really a matter of semantics. She considered the feedback and then chose to not change anything at this time, although she now has a nagging feeling as she plans math. This nagging feeling grows as she works with her Professional Learning Community (PLC) on shared math plans for the grade level. Ms. McCormick has entered the zone of Conscious Incompetence. Either way, Ms. McCormick has moved on the Conscious Competence Ladder.

Maslow probably wouldn't have agreed with the order of the Competence Ladder. Instead, I believe he would have lobbied for a different end goal: Conscious Competence. Once educators are in that learning space, their leaders can provide high-quality feedback that positions them to effectively autosupervise. High-quality written feedback, which demonstrates the desired outcomes delineated in Chapters 3–7, does not function as an "extrinsic satisfaction" (Maslow, 1973), rather it serves as the input self-actualizing people *need* to monitor their development and growth. If Maslow was giving Burch feedback, (high-quality written feedback, of course), he might suggest some arrow changes, as demonstrated by the revised matrix in Figure 2.6.

At the heart of these modifications is the notion that some educators build their practice first, then their beliefs might catch up (Choice 1 by Ms. McCormick). Other educators build their beliefs and eventually their practice is positively affected (Choice 2 by Ms. McCormick). In each case, the goal is Conscious Competence, a space where educators are clear about *what* they are doing and why they are doing *that*.

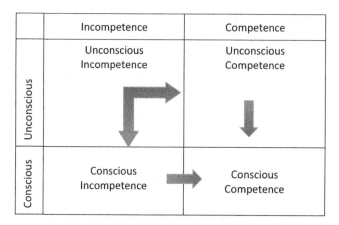

Figure 2.6   Revised Conscious Competence Matrix

Teaching and Hurdling

Although there probably could be a strong argument for a metaphor between teaching and hurdling, my experience tells me the metaphor would end up in Burch's camp rather than Maslow's. My hurdling coach wanted Unconscious Competence, but school leaders want Conscious Competence. Creating "automatic" teachers is not the goal of school improvement—creating more reflective practitioners is the goal. When we exhibit Unconscious Competence, we lack the memory to reflect on the experience, and thus cannot learn from it without assistance.

For athletes, game recordings fill this void. Athletes in individual sports (swimming, archery, track and field, golf) regularly video record themselves so they can analyze what moves they made that impacted their performance. Athletes in group sports (basketball, football, volleyball) also video record themselves, but for two reasons: analyzing individual moves and identifying the responses of the other team members.

Although video recording classrooms for personal professional development is not a new practice, it is still a rare one. Educators who take the risky step of watching themselves and their students on film are amazed by what they see and hear, translating their observations into tangible steps to accelerate changes in classroom practice, still with the same goal: Conscious Competence. This goal explicitly fuels the National Board for Professional Teaching Standards as the video recording analyses form the hallmark of their certification process.

I have heard numerous administrators and teachers talk about amazing teachers using phrases like the following:

- She's so good.
- It's just so natural for her.
- He was a born teacher.
- I wasn't sure what to write down. Nothing I could say could make him any better!

I disagree. Veterans still want feedback and want it frequently. These experienced educators have just resigned themselves to their current reality: observations are rare, feedback is worthless, and I need to figure out my own way to grow if I want to improve (Baker Van Soelen, 2008). Self-determination from some veterans comes in the forms of voluntary or required instructional planning, informal gatherings of teachers, electronic and virtual learning, and peer observations. We owe each of these teachers the gift of high-quality feedback. Without it, we are practicing inequity.

Instructional Leadership

The framework and assessment tool in this book will assist school leaders in efficiently crafting meaningful feedback for *each* teacher in the building, regardless of competence or consciousness. The quality of the feedback matters.

Wood and Killian (1998) argue that supervision and teacher evaluation do not contribute to school improvement and that we must "restructure supervision and teacher evaluation so they support teacher learning" (p. 54).

Fifteen years later, researchers found similar results when framed around instructional leadership. Their work was popularized through a *Washington Post* article by Valerie Strauss (2014) with the intriguing title "Should Principals Stop Visiting Classrooms?" In this study, three researchers followed 100 principals around for a school day, recording what they did. Their main finding about instructional leadership mirrors what we know to be true about learning: feedback is essential. They posit instructional leadership activities that don't provide meaningful feedback to teachers are not worth doing: "Feedback is essential. Instructional leadership activities that offer meaningful feedback to teachers may help. Those that don't, will not" (Grissom et al., 2013, p. 2).

Also present in their findings was a negative association between walkthroughs and student achievement. When pursued through interviews, principals admitted that teachers in their buildings did not view the feedback from walkthroughs as professional development opportunities.

Autosupervision

Well-designed feedback causes thinking. It doesn't do all the thinking for the receiver; instead it creates the conditions for them to productively make sense of their feedback and take any subsequent actions.

This book clearly delineates the skills necessary to create high-quality feedback, keeping in mind the feedback is not the ultimate goal.

Teachers who receive written feedback crafted with description (Chapter 3), conditional language (Chapter 4), consistent point of view (Chapter 5), explicit assumptions (Chapter 6), and careful attention to co-teaching (Chapter 7) will *use* the feedback—it's too good of a gift not to use. It is akin to a gift card to an ice cream store. Your willpower may be telling you to not avail yourself of the 50+ flavors, but the gift is too powerful.

Sally Zepeda, a scholar of instructional supervision for over 20 years, posed a unique term back in 1996: autosupervision (Zepeda et al.). "Videotape analysis of classroom events is one way to promote autosupervision, a self-directed and self-guided way for teachers to examine their own instructional practices" (p. 26).

My clients and I have re-tooled this word, autosupervision, disassociated from collecting electronic or digital video footage. Autosupervision, in this context, represents the act of individuals processing their high-quality written feedback and accelerating improvements in classroom practice. The "auto" here does not mean without thought, or involuntarily. Rather in this context, the "auto" means "self." The self, the teacher, is able to use the description, the conditional language, the consistent point of view, and the explicit assumptions to see and hear their classroom practice in different ways.

Teachers who autosupervise could be at any stage in Burch's Conscious Competence framework. It is not necessary to be consciously competent in order to benefit from high-quality feedback. In fact, the same high-quality written feedback could be interpreted by a teacher in each quadrant. The text in Table 2.1 indicates what a teacher characterized by each descriptor *for that part of their teaching practice* might say after reading this small feedback excerpt.

Each teacher benefits from the feedback, but some need more face-to-face or additional written feedback in order to decide how to move forward. Teachers demonstrating principles of Conscious Competence can autosupervise beautifully, reconsidering their practices in choosing what to continue doing, what to change, and what to stop.

A high school principal used Figure 2.7 to explain to his staff why they were changing the way observers write feedback.

Table 2.1 Observation Feedback Interpreted Four Ways

Written feedback: During the read-aloud, three students were drawing, four students were reading a different text, and the remainder of the students had their eyes forward (either on you or something else in the front of the room). When asked why they have read-alouds, three separate students said they did not know.

Unconscious Incompetence	Unconscious Competence
I have never really thought about what kids are doing during the read-aloud. It's really a time to decompress when they come in after recess.	*My kids know the rules during the read-aloud. I guess I better be more attentive about those four who were reading their own books.*
Conscious Incompetence	**Conscious Competence**
Well, this is better than what I had a week ago. I guess my talk with them about my expectations really helped. I'm surprised they didn't have an idea about why I read a book after recess. I thought it was obvious.	*I am so glad that a few students were drawing. When I reviewed the expectations of what it means to attend during read-aloud and that it is frustration-level text, drawing scenes from the chapter book was an option. I think I might set a timer during my next read-aloud and do a quick read of the room three minutes in to see who is doing what. I could also walk around while I read—I might try that, too.*

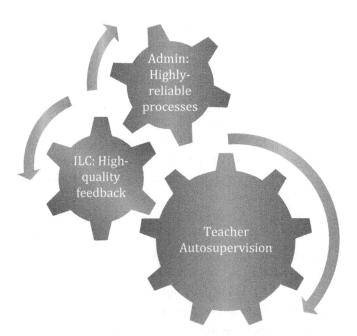

Figure 2.7 Visual Representing Changes in Teacher Evaluation Practices

Figure 2.7 represents the shorthand version of a Theory of Action:

If the administrators use highly reliable processes for each teacher in the building,

And if the processes are full of high-quality feedback crafted by the Instructional Leadership Team (ILC—assistant principals and department chairs),

And if this feedback is thoughtfully considered by the very teachers the feedback is designed to develop,

And if teachers note themselves benefiting and growing from the carefully crafted feedback,

Then teachers can autosupervise every time high-quality written feedback has been crafted.

Receiving Feedback

Although there are not many texts regarding how to craft written feedback, numerous authors have written about how to deliver feedback in person. Both business and education leaders have frameworks for leaders to use in preparing for and executing these conversations.

The author of the feedback, often the supervisor, is a person, and thus has a relationship with the observed. It is naïve to not consider this as an important factor. In fact, Stone and Heen (2014) include the relationship with the supervisor as one of three triggered reactions that can help us better accept the feedback.

Getting feedback from people you greatly respect, perhaps idolize, is like a home loan in 2008: preapproved. Now there's everybody else: the *them* bucket.

> Feedback from these others may not be pre*disqualified,* but we are on higher alert. We can disqualify the giver on any number of grounds—the most common involving trust, credibility, and the (lack of) skill or judgment with which they deliver their feedback. And once we disqualify the giver, we reject the substance of the feedback without a second thought. Based on the who, *we discard the* what.
>
> (Stone & Heen, 2014, p. 106, reprinted with permission)

This book focuses on developing the "skill" mentioned above. Once written feedback meets the criteria contained in Chapters 3–7, trust and credibility are outcomes.

Teacher Evaluation as Accountability

Teacher evaluation can be characterized by a few metaphors, the first two being limiting. The first, teacher evaluation as accountability, is most present in educational policy. Considerable time and effort is spent debating the merits of teacher evaluation systems that use student achievement as a component of a final teacher evaluation score. Significant federal government grant programs (e.g., Race to the Top, Teacher Incentive Fund) and No Child Left Behind waivers have heightened a stir that all contain hints of incentive-based pay.

Literature is available to districts seeking reliability, validity, and even fairness to their teaching evaluation processes. Educational giants like James Popham (2013) and Linda Darling-Hammond (2013) have weighed in, making sure their concerns are well-documented.

The focus on student achievement scores remains constant: 46 out of 50 states require or recommend that evaluation systems include measures of how teachers positively impact their students' achievement (Hull, 2013). Almost half (23) require or recommend that these measures comprise at least 50% of the evaluation.

These important policy conversations are über-focused on the multiple measures of teacher evaluation, particularly student achievement scores. This discussion occasionally discusses observation, but limits the discussion to inter-rater reliability. Chapter 3 offers greater detail about a larger concern: inter-observer agreement. Inter-rater reliability focuses on the evaluative rating or score while inter-observer agreement concentrates on whether each observer *saw* and *heard* the same thing in the classroom.

A system hyper-focused on inter-rater reliability believes that the rating words (e.g., Proficient, Needs Development) or rating score is the most important factor to determine success of the system. Systems that desire high inter-observer agreement seek to provide meaningful feedback. Observers that view classrooms similarly and feed the feedback back to teachers will experience more success.

Teacher Evaluation as Feedback

The second metaphor, teacher evaluation as feedback, poses a challenge in many places, as it is quite a leap for many teachers to consider their written narratives as helpful feedback. Their evaluation products have been so generalized or full of educational jargon they lack meaning. Feedback isn't feedback to the receiver unless she/he can make meaning from it.

Since there is a dearth of literature about the feedback quality in teacher evaluation systems, we can pursue what makes high-quality feedback for students.

Grant Wiggins (2012) successfully synthesizes high-quality feedback for students using these seven criteria:

1. Goal-referenced
2. Tangible and transparent
3. Actionable
4. User-friendly (specific and personalized)
5. Timely
6. Ongoing
7. Consistent

This book about writing feedback to adults maps quite well to these principles for students. Specifically, the following chapters align as detailed in Table 2.2.

Table 2.2 Student Feedback Mapped to Adult Feedback

Student Feedback	Adult Written Feedback
Goal-referenced	Chapter 3: Description
Tangible and transparent	Chapter 3: Description Chapter 6: Assumptions
Actionable	Chapter 4: Conditional Language
User-friendly (specific and personalized)	Chapter 3: Description Chapter 5: Point of View

The last three criteria are not explicitly addressed in this book; however, the skills learned in Chapters 3–7, when consistently used and honed, will result in timely and consistent feedback. Once you become consciously competent at these skills, the teachers you support will want you to provide this quality of feedback more often, thus meeting the remaining student feedback criterion: ongoing.

Modeling the very expectations we hold for student feedback is a strong instructional strategy. Teachers don't model for their own benefit—it impacts learning. The way school leaders explicitly model for their faculties creates the conditions where learning thrives. The recipients of the modeling, in this case the teachers, can immediately translate their experiences with other adults to their interactions with students.

Teacher Evaluation as School Improvement

When feedback products from teacher evaluation pervasively produce adult learning and development throughout an organization, then we have moved past *teacher evaluation as accountability* and *teacher evaluation as feedback*. The organization has entered *teacher evaluation as school improvement*. Only in this last iteration will meaningful teacher evaluation practices become a systemic input with long-lasting results.

Three building blocks for a learning organization have been articulated:

1. Supportive learning environment
2. Concrete learning processes and practices
3. Leadership behavior that reinforces learning (Garvin et al., 2008)

Written feedback *can* be the primary action of an instructional leader. Imagine listing teacher evaluation practices as an action in a school or campus improvement plan—and really meaning it.

As school and district leaders, we have been reticent because we lacked criteria to self-assess. Keep reading. Here they come.

Try It Yourself

1. Try the *Continuum Dialogue* (http://schoolreforminitiative.org/doc/continuum_dialogue.pdf) with staff. Consider gathering feedback on several schoolwide practices, including classroom observation feedback as one of many.

2. Make a 2 × 2 Conscious Competence matrix for your leadership practices. What responsibilities fall into each box? Offering this as a learning experience with other administrators in your building could yield very productive discussion.

3. Leverage the power of one-item surveys. Try one using an anonymous platform like Survey Monkey. Your first item: "Please rate the usefulness of the written feedback you receive from this school's leadership." A small Likert scale of 4 may obfuscate the problem, so ponder a scale with more iterations. A Likert scale of 1–6 is my personal favorite. Once you have the results, make the results public with your staff, and let them know what you are about to do. Chapter 8 includes some important actions to mull over with your staff as you make changes in your own practice. At the end of the year, give the one-item survey again.

4. Consider your learning from this chapter: What practices from this chapter are 10-degree changes? Which might require a 90-degree change in your practice? What might be first on your docket?

Reference List

Baker Van Soelen, J. (2008). Honoring the voices: Perspectives of veteran teachers on instructional supervision. In S.J. Zepeda (Ed.), *Real-World Supervision: Adapting Theory to Practice* (pp. 29–49). Norwood, MA: Christopher-Gordon Publishers.

Darling-Hammond, L. (2013). *Getting teacher evaluation right.* New York, NY: Teachers College Press.

Garvin, D.A., Edmondson, A.C., & Gino, F. (2008). Is Yours a Learning Organization? *Harvard Business Review, 86*(3), 109–16, 134.

Grissom, J.A., Loeb, S., & Master, B. (2013). Effective instructional time use for school leaders: Longitudinal evidence from observations of principals. *Educational Researcher, 42,* 433–444.

Hull, J. (2013). *Trends in teacher evaluation: How states are measuring teacher performance.* Center for Public Education, National School Boards Association, Reston, VA.

Maslow, A. (1973). *On dominance, self-esteem, and self-actualization.* Monterey, CA: Brooks/Cole.

Popham, W.J. (2013). *Evaluating America's teachers: Mission possible?* Thousand Oaks, CA: Corwin.

Stone, D., & Heen, S. (2014). *Thanks for the feedback: The art and science of receiving feedback well.* New York, NY: Random House.

Strauss, V. (January 8, 2014). Should principals stop visiting classrooms? *The Washington Post.* Retrieved from https://www.washingtonpost.com/news/answer-sheet/wp/2014/01/08/should-principals-stop-visiting-classrooms/.

Wiggins, G. (2012). Seven keys to effective feedback. *Educational Leadership, 70*(1), 10–16.

Wood, F.H., & Killian, J. (1998). Job-embedded learning makes the difference in school improvement. *Journal of Staff Development, 19*(1), 52–54.

Zepeda, S.J., Wood, F., & O'Hair, M.J. (1996). A vision of supervision for 21st century schooling: Trends to promote change inquiry, and reflection. *Wingspan, 11*(2), 26–30.

3

Building Your Descriptive Prowess

Language matters. The words we use provide a treasure-trove from which readers infer. As readers of adult fiction, we rely on the author's ability to paint a picture of the sunken ship, the desolate dystopian world, or the lush Irish countryside. Accomplished authors use techniques to transport us into the book's setting. Teachers of writing will coach their protégés to "add more description" or "rely on all [their] senses."

During my dissertation writing a decade ago, I used the methodology of portraiture (Lawrence-Lightfoot, 1997) to fully describe a novice learning community. A period novel by Ernest Gaines (1983) about southern race relations became a mentor text. Here is a sample of descriptive text from *A Gathering of Old Men:*

> Yank was in his early seventies, but he still thought he was a cowboy. He used to break horses and mules thirty, forty years ago, and he still wore the same kinda clothes he wore back then. His straw hat was draped like a cowboy hat. Wore a faded red polka-dotted handkerchief, tied in a loose knot round his neck. His pants legs was stucked down in his rubber boots—not cowboy boots. Back, shoulders had been broke I don't know how many times; made him walk leaning forward. Hands had been broke and rebroke; now he couldn't shut them too tight, or open them too wide. But he still thought he was a cowboy.
>
> (p. 41, reprinted with permission of the publisher)

Although I certainly do not purport that written classroom feedback should be fictitious, learning how to provide rich description is a transferable skill. In the form of writing we use for teacher evaluation (nonfiction/informational/expository), we chronicle what is seen and heard with fewer subjective adjectives.

> *The field contained abundant rows of red tulips, yearning to be harvested.*

This sentence leaves us with questions: How much does it take for a field to be "abundant"? How might I look at a tulip to know if it is "yearning" to be harvested? If we focused solely on what we could see and hear, it might sound like the following:

> *The ¼-acre field contained 40 rows of red tulips. The petal tips were still touching on the plants at the ends of the rows.*

As teachers read feedback collected in their classrooms, they should be able to picture themselves there, what they said, what their students said, what happened when. The lush word choice should not be the propellant that causes teachers to relive those moments; rather it should be the *accuracy* of what was collected.

Play-by-Play Commentator

> *Mrs. Jackson, you have a lovely way with your students. It is clear they both respect and appreciate you. Even though you are teaching repeaters for Math 6, an observer would never know it from your interactions and their responses. Keep it up!*

When I was in elementary school, my father was a college athletic director and coach. Sometimes I attended games and matches, other times the college radio station provided everything we needed. After my mother would negotiate the fuzz around 88.5 FM, the play-by-play commentator painted the necessary picture, often with a speed that required close listening.

It's Dykstra on the top. Passed off to Jensen on the right side. Bounce pass back to Dykstra at the three-point line. Two dribbles in, stopped by double-team. Hands are up—Walhof comes over from the other side. Walhof dribbling back left, lob into Rylaarsdam. He turns, jump shot, bank—and in!

Nothing frilly or extra in the description—just the facts. I can picture myself there, in the gymnasium, watching through the power of language. That is the gift of the play-by-play commentator. To him, it's his job, but to the listener, it provides unfiltered access to the experience.

Mrs. Jackson may have smiled as she received her feedback about her Math 6 class. The smile may have been a smirk of relief or genuine gratitude to her principal. However, I wouldn't qualify those few sentences as high-quality feedback because the narrative doesn't meet the end-product test: the feedback didn't cause *thinking*. What would have been better for this hard-working teacher is a narrative full of rich description that helps her formatively assess, that is, *make a decision* about what to replicate and what to stop doing.

Inter-Observer Agreement

In working with a large comprehensive high school of 3,500 students, Principal Bo Ford took the first step: acknowledging the number one skill his leaders needed was to increase the quality of their classroom observation narratives. With 23 observers (11 assistant principals, 11 department chairs, and himself), he knew there was great room for inequity.

He wanted to check for inter-rater reliability and knew it was important. Linda Darling-Hammond (2013) describes how the Teacher Advancement Program gathers inter-rater reliability data from observers as feedback about the clarity of their rubrics. Any variants in quality are consistently focused back on the rubrics themselves. What this practice might assume is that two observers' evidence is of similar quality. That is an assumption I have found to be quite tenuous.

James Popham, testing expert, addresses four threats to rating accuracy in *Evaluating America's Teachers: Mission Possible?* (2013):

1. Severity error—predisposition to supply lower ratings than the rater would have given if no bias had been present, will lean lower if on the border between two categories

2. Generosity error—predisposition to supply higher ratings than the rater would have given if no bias had been present, will lean higher if on the border between two categories

3. Central-tendency error—predisposition to supply mid-quality ratings irrespective of performance; play it safe don't offend

4. Halo effect—single, particularly noteworthy dimension affects the entire assessment regardless of evidence

(pp. 122–123. *Evaluating America's Teachers* by Popham, W. [William] James, reproduced with permission of Corwin in the format, republished in a book via Copyright Clearance Center.)

Popham notes, "What we are hoping for, of course, is that when different observers watch the same actions of a teacher and the teacher's students, those observers will end up recording essentially the same events" (2013, p. 103). This standard moves leaders past seeking inter-rater reliability. The new, more rigorous goal is inter-observer agreement. Did we actually see and hear the same things? Only then can we have a conversation about what the evidence means in terms of our rating scales.

Principal Ford had been checking for inter-rater reliability in typical ways:

1. "Unpacking" each teaching standard and asking fellow observers what that really looked like and sounded like in classrooms

2. Watching short video clips with leaders and asking them to evaluate the clip using the 4-point rating scale

3. Pairing up and observing a live classroom for a few minutes, leaving the room, and negotiating which rating is most apropos

All of these are highly effective practices to develop inter-rater reliability. However, he was not reaching his stated goal to his leaders: "We need to be more objective and have less bias." The root cause of the inequity in the quality of the narratives was not about the rating; it was about what was collected during the observation. In Popham's words, the inter-observer accuracy was shaky.

Rich description provides the evidence needed to build a shared understanding about what was really seen and heard. Only through that evidence-based talk can ratings be appropriately assigned.

I liken that experience to school leaders who, full of trepidation, open the envelope or electronic file with their state assessment scores. With other trusted colleagues they take a breath and look. It usually takes less than 10 seconds before someone says, "Whoa. What are we going to do about _____?" The blank might be "math" or "science." No description occurs in these moments—it is an immediate jump to emotion and opinion. The others in the room don't even know what the speaker is referring to: Math for all students? Math for one demographic group? The math percentage pass? The scale score? We do not have a shared understanding about what we are looking at, much less agreement about the questions raised.

After a 30-minute professional development experience about description with each of Principal Ford's observers, this "ticket out the door" was offered:

> *Please watch this three-minute video clip and type into the Google form URL link the answer to this question: What did you see and hear in this classroom?*

Table 3.1 represents the range of description (rich to sparse) evident in a room of school leaders.

Even in a short three minutes, the data from this group of leaders is quite telling and ripe to be used in a formative way:

- One observer wrote only three words in three minutes.
- The word "lots" appears four times.
- Two observers quantified something (e.g., "three students").
- Three observers used direct quotations.
- Evaluative language appears in more than 50% of the responses (e.g., "really," "noisy," "a lot").

If you were confused by the response in the third row, second column ("3.1, 3.2, 3.6"), you are in good company. The teachers in this assistant principal's academic department were confused, too. They eventually figured out that this coding system referred to the list of sample actions present in the new teacher evaluation system. Interestingly enough, another leader in the room viewed the video in similar ways and produced his

Table 3.1 Range of Description

kid in blue hoodie seems to write entire time but never looks up oral response seems to come from only one, possible two kids every time kids pay attention when teacher runs out and in	prompting questions to check for understanding lots of energy interest	voice has varied inflection and tone, back to at least one student while speaking, moves around the classroom in the beginning rather than standing in one place, uses a power point with a visual, uses classroom door to demonstrate difference between pro-slavery and anti-slavery
energetic. running in and out. movement. yelling out questions. "I am a what?" he asks lots of questions. back is to the kid behind him. "This is an African American gentleman who is asked to . . ." foreshadowing . . . Like a mad lib . . . lots to "fill in"	Teacher has left the room by giving active example. Teacher moving around a lot. Some students not looking at all that he is doing. His back is to several students and they are not watching him. Using visual representation with pointer to point things out. Talks really fast and loud.	Interactive classroom. Students responding to questions from teacher. Lots of movement in/out of the classroom. Using a pointer to point out specifics in the picture on the screen. Moving in and out of the rows of students. Students answering questions out loud—not needing to be called on.
Mr. Adams moved in and out of the room to describe pro-slavery and anti-slavery people in a historical perspective. Mr. Adams asked questions and paused to wait for students to fill in the blanks. Sometimes he waited for answers and sometimes he supplied them and talked over the student answers.	3.1 3.2 3.6	Engages students in active learning and maintains interest. Builds upon students' existing knowledge and skills. Communicates and presents material clearly, and checks for understanding.

Had a ppt and a clicker to help explain John Brown. Showed the confederate and union flags in the picture— "Show foreshadowing of what is to come"		
knowledgeable in subject area asking for feedback using technology	*Energy dramatic Goal?*	*Playing "guess the word in my head." Somewhat noisy Teacher was in and out of classroom. Used powerpoint and visuals Laser pointer*
3 students writing, not participating in dialogue. Use of door entry was very dramatic, however the metaphor may not have been received by all. Very enthusiastic teaching style, had three students to your back when lecturing.	*Teacher ran in and out of room to try and help students "remember" the point of descriptions in lecture. Technology was used by displaying the picture of historical people and time being described. Students in varying degrees of attentiveness. One on front row was especially visually engaged, another writing (but not sure about what).*	*Very animated. Notes oral. Notes flashed away (Bleeding Kansas) very quickly as he went to the picture of John Brown. Teacher provided the interpretation of the picture. Students given no chance to participate. Pace was quick, it would be difficult for special need students to take notes in the time provided.*

feedback in the third column, third row. These three statements were copied and pasted from sample actions 3.1, 3.2, and 3.6 found in the teacher evaluation system manual.

As you can see, a roomful of experienced, dedicated educators did not and cannot automatically and successfully describe what they see and hear without venturing into interpretation and evaluation. Tina Blythe and her colleagues offer ideas about why this might be the case:

> I suspect that two tendencies in our culture mix dangerously and make what should be a simple act of description far more difficult than one might anticipate. First, we tend to move very quickly and rarely stop to dwell at length on what is before our eyes. A trip to a museum to watch people looking at the art often confirms that most of us spend very little time looking at a single painting. Face to face with a Rembrandt, an extraordinary opportunity to observe the work of a master, to dwell on what many consider a major accomplissment of Western culture . . . most of us spend little more than a minute or two.
>
> Further, we seem to be in the habit of making very quick judgments, even of things that might benefit from some reflection. We often expect of ourselves and our companions that we will know our thoughts, feelings, and opinions of a film before we've even crossed the street outside the theater. Exemplified by the film critics' Siskel and Ebert's "thumbs up" or "thumbs down," there is a "let's look at it once, declare it good or bad, and get onto the next" mentality that dominates our behavior perhaps a bit more than we might like to admit.
>
> (pp. 30–31. Reprinted with permission of the publisher. From Tina Blythe, David Allen, and Barbara Schieffelin Powell, *Looking Together at Student Work,* 2nd Edition, New York: Teachers College Press. Copyright © 2008 by Tina Blythe, David Allen, and Barbara S. Powell. All rights reserved.)

Although Siskel and Ebert is a reference less commonplace in 2015, Facebook is not. Imagine an observer giving a classroom a "Like" each time she/he exits. Using primarily evaluative written feedback is akin to that very move.

DIE: An Acronym Worth Remembering

That being said, description *is* a skill to be learned. A first step when co-observers walk out of a classroom or when "Stop" has been pushed on a video clip is *not* to ask what you want to ask: "What do you think?" Reframing this question to "What did we see and hear?" makes a significant difference on the breadth and depth of evidence provided to teachers.

However, a new question does not a new behavior make. Description must be practiced, not only in classrooms but in other contexts, too. Educators engaged in the School Reform Initiative critical friendship, a particular kind of professional learning community, use descriptive protocols to seek perspective on work they have created (e.g., a plan, a letter, a brochure, a set of belief statements) or the work of their students (e.g., a piece of writing, some artwork, an electronic product).

In 1988, Steve Seidel and his colleagues at Harvard's Project Zero (Blythe et al., 2008) developed a collaborative process to analyze students' products, in search of better understandings about students' thinking, which in turn inform teacher's next steps for instruction.

One protocol that groups can use to capture their collective thinking about these products is called the *Collaborative Assessment Conference* (Blythe et al., 2008). In this experience, educators methodically examine the artifacts, slowing down adults' thinking as they speak about one dimension at a time.

Collaborative Assessment Conference

1. Getting Started
   a. The group chooses a facilitator who will make sure the group stays focused on the particular issue addressed in each step.
   b. The presenting teacher puts the selected work in a place where everyone can see it or provides copies for the other participants. She/he says nothing about the work, the context in which it was created, or the student, until Step 5.
   c. The participants observe or read the work in silence, perhaps making brief notes about aspects of it that they particularly notice.

---

2. Describing the Work

   a. The facilitator asks the group: "What do you see?"

   b. Group members provide answers without making judgments about the quality of the work or their personal preferences.

   c. If a judgment emerges, the facilitator asks for the evidence on which the judgment is based.

3. Asing Questions About the Work

   a. The facilitator asks the group: "What questions does this work raise for you?"

   b. Group members state any questions they have about the work, the child, the assignment, the circumstances under which the work was carried out, and so on.

   c. The presenting teacher may choose to make notes about these questions, but she/he does not respond to them now—nor is she/he obligated to respond to them in Step 5 during the time when the presenting teacher speaks.

4. Speculating About What the Student Is Working On

   a. The facilitator asks the group, "What do you think the child is working on?"

   b. Participants, based on their reading or observation of the work, make suggestions about the problems or issues that the student might have been focused on in carrying out the assignment.

5. Hearing From the Presenting Teacher

   a. The facilitator invites the presenting teacher to speak.

   b. The presenting teacher provides his or her perspective on the student's work, describing what she/he sees in it, responding (if she/he chooses) to one or more of the questions raised, and adding any other information that she/he feels is important to share with the group.

   c. The presenting teacher also comments on anything surprising or unexpected that she/he heard during the describing, questioning, and speculating phases.

6. Discussing Implications for Teaching and Learning

> The facilitator invites everyone (the participants and the presenting teacher) to share any thoughts they have about their own teaching, children's learning, or ways to support this particular child in future instruction.

7. Reflecting on the Collaborative Assessment Conference

> The group reflects on the experiences of the conference as a whole or particular parts of it.

Reprinted with permission of the publisher. From Tina Blythe, David Allen, and Barbara Schieffelin Powell, *Looking Together at Student Work,* 2nd Edition, New York: Teachers College Press. Copyright © 2008 by Tina Blythe, David Allen, and Barbara S. Powell. All rights reserved.

Although the steps are distinct, they can be clustered using the three ways of looking described in *Looking Together at Student Work* (Blythe et al., 2008): description, interpretation, evaluation. Table 3.2 presents an alignment of these three concepts to the protocol.

Table 3.2 Aligning the *Collaborative Assessment Conference* to Description, Interpretation, and Evaluation

Step 2: Describing the Work	Description
Step 3: Asking Questions About the Work	Interpretation
Step 4: Speculating About What the Student Is Working On	Interpretation
Step 6: Discussing Implications for Teaching and Learning	Evaluation (of our learning, not of the student's work)

Blythe and her colleagues use very clear language to help educators discriminate between the three terms:

> *Description:* involves identifying in very literal terms what constitutes the piece of work being observed

Interpretation: involves assigning some meaning or intent to what is in the work

Evaluation: attaches value or personal preference to the work being examined

(Reprinted with permission of the publisher. From Tina Blythe, David Allen, and Barbara Schieffelin Powell, *Looking Together at Student Work,* 2nd Edition, New York: Teachers College Press. Copyright © 2008 by Tina Blythe, David Allen, and Barbara S. Powell. All rights reserved.)

Using a piece of student-generated artwork, the following demonstrates what each of the three ways of looking would sound like:

Description: I see a yellow circle.
Interpretation: There's a sun in a deep blue sky.
Evaluation: The sun is drawn skillfully.

(Reprinted with permission of the publisher. From Tina Blythe, David Allen, and Barbara Schieffelin Powell, *Looking Together at Student Work,* 2nd Edition, New York: Teachers College Press. Copyright © 2008 by Tina Blythe, David Allen, and Barbara S. Powell. All rights reserved.)

Perhaps you've already anticipated this: these three ways of looking form an unfortunate, but memorable acronym: DIE. Being clear when our feedback falls into which concept is critical to the success of using descriptive language.

Innovation Configuration Map

This desired outcome of **Description** on the Innovation Configuration Map includes descriptions of each variation as well as sample text. The least acceptable option, noted in Table 3.3 as Level 4, uses two criteria: the subject of the feedback and the quality of the feedback.

Similar to the shift in the last decade from teaching to learning, observation practices have begun to shift from watching and listening to *adults* to watching and listening to *students.* This is particularly evident in walkthrough forms, which began as primarily environmental observations

Table 3.3 Desired Outcome: Description on the High-Quality Feedback Innovation Configuration Map

	1	2	3	4
Description *Purpose:* *to see and* *hear what's* *going on in a* *classroom*	Feedback is highly **descriptive,** balancing rich descriptions of student behaviors and teacher behaviors. Feedback includes **data** that was seen and heard, using direct **quotations** when appropriate. *"Three students put their heads down during the 10-minute movie, near the 6-minute mark. You remained at the back of the room speaking once to a student. It appeared that 10 students wrote something down. One student near the door used a Flow Map."*	Feedback is mostly **descriptive,** including **approximations** for what was seen and/or heard. Feedback may include student behaviors as well as teacher behaviors. *"Three students slept during the 10-minute movie. You remained at the back of the room watching the movie with the students."*	Feedback uses primarily **evaluative** and **interpretive** language. Feedback may include student behaviors as well as teacher behaviors. *"Students appeared off-task and bored during the movie despite your directions for them to take notes."*	Feedback primarily draws on **evaluative** language. Feedback is limited to teacher behaviors. *"You allowed the sleeping students too long before you intervened."*

(e.g., standards posted, desks in clusters, word wall posted), were revised to focus more on teaching behaviors (e.g., teacher circulating room, what were the responses to inaccurate answers), and were revised again to collect the behaviors and actions of the learners (e.g., what students were doing, what students said they were to be learning).

Level 4 Feedback

Level 4 feedback (Table 3.4) does not match the purpose of this desired outcome: *to see and hear what's going on in a classroom.* The observer may have met this purpose prior to writing the feedback but the reader, the teacher, is unclear. By relying on evaluative feedback, the reader must ascertain what evidence, if any, the observer used to make their assertions. Although this feedback does meet the litmus test of asking the receiver to think about the feedback, this cognitive energy is misplaced. It would be far more productive for teachers to use diligently collected descriptive feedback as another set of eyes and ears in their classroom.

Consider the feedback in Table 3.5. Keep in mind the definition shared earlier—*evaluation:* attached value or personal preference to the

Table 3.4 Description: Level 4 Feedback

	1	2	3	4
Description *Purpose:* to see and hear what's going on in a classroom				Feedback primarily draws on **evaluative** language. Feedback is limited to teacher behaviors. *"You allowed the sleeping students too long before you intervened."*

Table 3.5 Level 4 Feedback and Something Better

Level 4 Feedback	Better Iteration
The groups were *too noisy* and *unfocused. I prefer* for each group member to have a specific role. This prevents the chaos I saw today.	All five groups of students needed more than one redirection during the observation. Four times the expression, "Quiet down, folks!" was used. Students understood what their product needed to be as evidenced by student responses to questions. However, it is unclear from the direction sheet and asking students if they knew their expectations as a group and as individuals.

work being examined. The *italicized* text in the table indicates the evidence placing this feedback in Level 4.

As we more frequently notice evaluative language in our own writing and speaking, we become more aligned with the expectations we have set for teachers in their work with students. Of seven best practices for offering feedback to students (Wiggins, 2012), goal-referenced and tangible are two specifics. Evaluative language can muddle the goal and create a dependency on the feedback giver to mark progress, resulting in learned helplessness.

Level 3 Feedback

Level 3 feedback (Table 3.6) demonstrates evidence from teachers and students and contains both interpretive and evaluative language. Remember the definitions from earlier:

> *Interpretation:* involves assigning some meaning or intent to what is in the work
> *Evaluation:* attaches value or personal preference to the work being examined.

The *italicized* text in the table indicates the evidence placing this feedback in Level 3.

Table 3.6 Description: Level 3 Feedback

	1	2	3	4
Description *Purpose:* to see and hear what's going on in a classroom			Feedback uses primarily **evaluative** and **interpretive** language. Feedback may include student behaviors as well as teacher behaviors. *"Students appeared off-task and bored during the movie despite your directions for them to take notes."*	Feedback primarily draws on **evaluative** language. Feedback is limited to teacher behaviors. *"You allowed the sleeping students too long before you intervened."*

Table 3.7 Level 3 Feedback and Something Better

Level 3 Feedback	Better Iteration
Students *were confused* by the graphic organizer. *Since it wasn't exactly the same as the one modeled for them, they weren't sure what to do. The new organizer may have assessed their ability to translate their learning, which is great! I really liked that part.* An exemplar would have helped.	100% of the questions asked by students during the observation were about the graphic organizer, particularly Part II that was different from the previous organizer they had used. Sometimes students walked around, following you as you circulated, other times raising their hands. "I don't understand this box." "What am I supposed to do here?"

"I really liked that part." Notice how this text is italicized in Table 3.7 thus selected as evidence placing this feedback iteration in Level 3. Providing praise is a tricky proposition. Although some writers encourage starting off feedback sessions with praise (Bambrick-Santoyo, 2012), it is generally discouraged in most coaching literature. As soon as "I like" or "It was great when . . ." begins a sentence, the E of DIE emerges. Although that seems innocuous to start with praise, something positive, it is risky. The risk comes from the fact that we dove into the deep end of the pool (Evaluation) without first making sure we both felt and agreed on the temperature of the water (Description).

Most times the intention of praise matches with the result. A parent eagerly and loudly praises his child after an excellent corner kick in soccer. The child runs just a bit faster down the field after the next exchange. A piano teacher notices her young charge has curved his fingers for the first time without being reminded and praises him. During the rest of the lesson, the teacher never had to remind him—not even once.

With written feedback, praise is misplaced. Without the in-person interaction to assess whether the intention matches the result, the risk is too high. Consider this feedback offered to a middle school teacher:

> You had a variety of instructional activities included in the lesson. You had your EQ and activities clearly displayed on the board. You clearly put a lot of thought and deliberate planning into your lessons. I appreciate your hard work!

After the observation and before the written feedback was received, Mrs. Tillery was worried. This unannounced visit took her by surprise and she wasn't at all happy with how it went. Her mother entered the hospital last Friday, which certainly put a hiccup in her intentions to write lesson plans for the next week.

After partaking in a special drink in a special glass after her own children were in bed, she opens her teacher evaluation portal and downloads the feedback document. An audible laugh—technically a guffaw—emanates from her body as she begins to read. Her husband leaves his desk to come check. As she is still laughing and blinking back tears—probably from a mix of stressors, she offers, "It's just my evaluation. I always get so worked up, and it clearly doesn't matter. My principal read the whiteboard which I hadn't erased from last week and assumed I had lesson plans. In fact, he rated me as Exemplary!"

After a few more sips, a few more tears, and a tissue or two, Mrs. Tillery opens her lesson plan book. Staring at the blank boxes for the current week, she gently closes it and murmurs, "I guess it isn't as important to him

Table 3.8 Sample Data Collection Headings

Positive	Negative
Glow	Grow
+	Δ
Appreciate	Wonder
Impressed	Implore
Strengths	Challenges

as I thought it was." The principal has unwittingly lowered a teacher's own expectations to better match her perception of his.

The interpretive *(a lot, deliberate)* and evaluative *(hard work)* language is easy to spot in the principal's well-meaning feedback. Sometimes the document itself is what posits a clearly evaluative stance. I've seen each pair of words in Table 3.8 appear on data collection forms. All represent variations on a theme.

Each of these T-charts start in the deep end of the pool. No matter what words are used, it will be quite difficult for the reader to believe that there is a desire to first come to agreement on what was seen and heard.

Level 2 Feedback

After focusing on description, many school leaders can reach Level 2 feedback (Table 3.9). Their written products start to elongate as they are documenting many more behaviors of students and teachers. They have become more cognizant of interpretive and evaluative language creeping into their narratives. Using time as a marker becomes more commonplace. Leaders with backgrounds in special education often call forth those data collection skills.

Level 2 feedback is acceptable. Notice that although it is to the right of the ideal boldface line, it is not grayscaled. This amount and quality of description can be helpful to teachers as they attempt to recollect their lesson while reading your version. Table 3.10 offers an example of such Level 2 feedback.

In any cycle of improvement, we check in on our development along the way. These might be called formative checks in a classroom or leading

Table 3.9 Description: Level 2 Feedback

	1	2	3	4
Description *Purpose:* to see and hear what's going on in a classroom		Feedback is mostly **descriptive,** including **approximations** for what was seen and/ or heard. Feedback may include student behaviors as well as teacher behaviors. *"Three students slept during the 10-minute movie. You remained at the back of the room watching the movie with the students."*	Feedback uses primarily **evaluative** and **interpretive** language. Feedback may include student behaviors as well as teacher behaviors. *"Students appeared off-task and bored during the movie despite your directions for them to take notes."*	Feedback primarily draws on **evaluative** language. Feedback is limited to teacher behaviors. *"You allowed the sleeping students too long before you intervened."*

indicators in a school improvement plan. A marker can be set for description, too.

Figure 3.1 represents how to assess the feedback gathered *during* the classroom observation itself.

One hundred percent of the time spent during a classroom observation should be spent in descriptive mode. As you sit on a hard chair, a plastic stool, or even a bean bag, any moments that are spent wondering about root causes, creating coaching language, or offering other strategies for the teacher to consider are all moments *not* spent collecting data. Without a storehouse of collected data, any interpretations or evaluative statements lack support.

Teachers of writing consistently tell their students to support their ideas. The Common Core State Standards transition from persuasive writing to argumentative writing in grades 6–12 has heightened the need for students to argue cogently with claims, evidence, and reasons. Leaders

Table 3.10 Level 2 Feedback and Something Better

Level 2 Feedback	Better Iteration
Students received a new math practice book about 3D objects. Actual 3D objects from the room were shown to students.	Students were introduced to a new math practice book, with the first page including content about 3D shapes. 3D objects from the room were shown to students as they examined the 2D picture of a 3D object.
Students were quite jazzed, wanting to participate. When you saw that they were bordering on being out of control, numbers were pulled from a cup. When students answered correctly, they received high fives.	Students were excitedly involved in the lesson, as evidenced by multiple hands raised. When too many "shout outs" occurred, numbers were used to balance participation. Almost every student who answered a question correctly received a high five.
When students were unclear about whether two objects on the workbook page were *both* spheres, a large and small sphere in the room were found. Some students held the spheres in the front of the room and a comparison was made to "big world we live in—could we have the same shape?"	When students were unclear about whether two objects on the workbook page were *both* spheres, a large and small sphere in the room were found. Two students held the spheres in the front of the room and a comparison was made to "big world we live in—could we have the same shape?" This misconception about size related to shape identification will probably surface throughout the whole unit due to their age, so it will be interesting to hear how you try to debunk that misunderstanding.
Students were informed that new vocabulary would be used today (e.g., rectangular prism, sphere, cone, cube, cylinder). When a student answered a question about what made a cylinder, he was asked, "How do you know?" The answer was textbook: "There are circles, but it is 3D." As the observation closed, students were engaged in conversation about what makes something 3D.	Students were informed that new vocabulary would be used today (e.g., rectangular prism, sphere, cone, cube, cylinder). When a student answered a question about what made a cylinder, he was asked, "How do you know?" The answer was textbook: "There are circles, but it is 3D." As the observation closed, students were engaged in a whole group conversation about what makes something 3D.

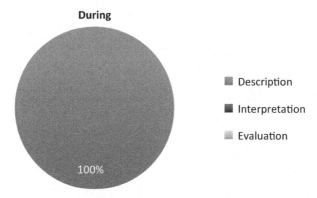

During

Description
Interpretation
Evaluation

100%

Figure 3.1 Focus During the Observation

often do not hold themselves to these same standards as they write classroom observation feedback. I suspect a teacher of writing would have much to say if she analyzed and assessed an observation narrative from an administrator. I can imagine the red pen!

A metaphor to keep in mind is a house. Description forms the walls while interpretation and evaluation compose the roof. A roof made of lightweight shingles has different weight-bearing specifications than a roof composed of Spanish tile. Similarly tough-to-hear interpretive or evaluative statements need numerous strong walls in order for the roof to stand in the mind of the reader, the teacher.

Once the observation is complete, interpretive and evaluative statements may be added but not to the detriment of the high-quality description. I have found that reflective teachers want a higher ratio of description compared to anything else—and not by just a little.

The Sci Academy, a new school birthed out of the remnants of Hurricane Katrina in New Orleans, innovates using Carol Dweck's growth mindset framework. They have documented success with primarily low-income students, including a 100% graduation rate, 97% to four-year colleges. A necessary feature of this success for the adults is a rigorous teacher development program. Alexie Gaddis, a math teacher, describes the feedback she receives from her coach: "I have a snapshot of what was going on in my classroom as soon as she leaves. That is a big factor in me being able to understand what is going on in my classroom on my own" (TeachForAll, 2013).

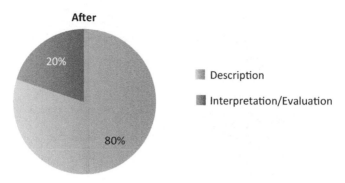

After

20%

80%

■ Description

■ Interpretation/Evaluation

Figure 3.2 Focus After the Observation

The 100% descriptive document we created while we were in the classroom can now be revised, adding some interpretation and/or evaluation (Figure 3.2). In practical terms, one nondescriptive statement generally needs four descriptive statements to support it—to be the walls so the roof doesn't crash to the ground.

Using description is not limited to just classroom observations. Consider this feedback written for a teacher after an observation of a Professional Learning Community meeting:

> *During the PLC, an assessment was brought for examination. This draft was created by a colleague who was seeking feedback. Over 30 pieces of feedback were given during the discussion, eight of which emanated from you. All eight of those inputs were derogatory of the assessment. Example responses include the following:*

- *"This question doesn't do anything."*
- *"Way too many questions about covalent bonds."*
- *"This graphic isn't helpful."*

Chapter 4 will assist feedback writers in determining what to write next after collecting this kind of evidence.

Is Description Feedback?

This is what a middle school assistant principal asked me after several hours of learning: "So then, is description really feedback or not?" Absolutely.

Feedback is receiving information about the performance of a task that can be used to improve.

These common occurrences in schools all meet this feedback definition:

- A performing arts group listens to or watches their recent performance.
- A sports team watches game/match video recording.
- During a showing of their morning show, members of the video production class note the expressions and comments of their homeroom classmates.

A word like "description" can even benefit from some unpacking. Principal Shannon Kersey knew that shared understandings about terms would be critical for her leadership team to successfully shift to more descriptive feedback. After spending a meeting watching videos and publicly sharing their descriptive attempts, the team created a T-chart capturing what they wanted to do more of and less of in their feedback. Their "more of" side included the following:

- Quotations from teacher(s)
- Quotations from students
- Quantify whenever possible (e.g., tally)
- First letter of student names when known
- Times and durations

All of these skills are learned and can be honed through repeated practice and cycles of feedback (on the feedback). It is very clear that a proper metaphor for teacher evaluator is not judge nor jury; instead, a more apt image is that of a data collector—a voracious, hard-working data collector.

Table 3.11 represents Dr. Edgar Karrell in a striking before and after. Dr. Karrell prided himself at summarizing well. He had the old teacher evaluation system down pat—a word document of favorite lines and quips were fodder as he completed his necessary evaluations. "Don't get me wrong," defends Dr. Karrell, "I did way more observations than what it says in here. Those were just walkthroughs and I don't provide feedback on those . . . unless I have to."

After co-observing, and comparing our narrative products after five minutes, Dr. Karrell agreed that his summary statements do not produce

Table 3.11 Dr. Karrell's Before and After

Before	After
Students were on the carpet listening to a nursery rhyme.	There are 20 students sitting on the carpet looking at the poem, "Little Boy Blue," on a colored chart. This nursery rhyme is being used to teach rhyming. The student teacher was sitting on a chair watching instruction. Sample responses to students: ● "We are listening for something that rhymes with horn." ● "What do you think, E?" ● When students spoke out loud without being called on: "It's C's turn, let's listen to C." Two moments of a formative strategy: 1. "If you think these two words rhyme, put both hands on your head." All students but one put their hands on their head. "M, why are both hands on top of your head?" Students saw a model of both hands on an adult head. 2. "If you think that X rhymes with Y, put your pinky on your nose." Students saw a model of a pinky on a nose. "Why do you have your pinky on your nose? . . . because my pinky is on my nose, so you did it too?" One attribute of rhyming words was offered: "Rhyming words are different at the beginning." It is unclear whether this "difference" was about the sound or the actual letter. A student added another attribute: "both words have the same sound at the end."

conditions necessary for teachers to learn from observations. He set a goal to sharpen his observation skills. "Too bad I can't type any faster with these fat fingers," he laments.

Note the use of bullets in the After iteration. At the beginning of my own journey in improving my feedback, I relied on a chronological account in each classroom. That made sense for me then, but as I became more confident in my descriptive skills, I realized that grouping and chunking the data was far more helpful for the reader, the teacher. "Sample responses to students" is an example of an organizational structure. Other structures I have used include the following:

- Questions asked that all begin with "what"
- Responses after students offered wrong answers to questions raised
- Responses to students of color
- Phrases that include highly affectionate group terms ("pumpkins," "babies," "dearies")
- Sample topics students were discussing during group work

Unknowingly, I was using two of the three functions of paraphrasing (Table 3.12) proffered by cognitive coaching theorists (Costa & Garmston, 2014).

Table 3.12 Paraphrasing Functions

Acknowledge and clarify	Summarize and organize	Shift levels of abstraction
- You're thinking that . . . - So you're wondering if . . . - You're frustrated because . . . - You're hoping that - You're concerned about . . .	- So, there are three issues . . . - You have closure on ___ and you're ready to move to _____ - You are wrestling with two competing notions. One . . . - First, you're going to ___ then you will _____/ - On one hand, . . . On the other hand . . .	- So, it's important to you that - So, a belief that you hold is - So, you're struggling with differentiation. - An assumption you might hold is . . . - An example of what you're talking about is - Something this is *not* about is . . .

Adapted from Costa, A.L., Garmston, R.J., Ellison, J., & Hayes, C. (2014). *Cognitive Coaching Foundation Seminars® Learning Guide* (10th ed.). Highlands Ranch, CO: Thinking Collaborative.

Although this framework is designed for 1:1 live interactions, the concepts transfer well to written feedback. The **acknowledge** came through the methodical documentation of what I saw and heard (description) and the **organize** is evidenced by the grouping of similar descriptions. The final paraphrasing category, **Shift levels of abstraction,** is evidenced in Chapter 6, "Explicitly Owning and Raising Assumptions."

Is It Worth It?

The Wallace Foundation has heavily invested in research identifying the link between effective leadership and student achievement. A video series entitled *School Leadership in Action: Principal Practices* (2015) featured principals who identify the qualities they find critical to improve teaching and learning. The fifth attribute, "Managing People, Data, and Processes," shows Principal Clayborn Knight observing Jon-Paul Coutourier. Mr. Coutourier draws a firm link between Knight's feedback and improvements in his classroom: "His notes are so thorough and detailed that you know for a fact, that he saw everything that was going on in the room."

Describing classrooms is hard work. It requires discipline to stay focused. Administrators multi-tasking is often treated as a badge of honor or a stripe of proficiency. In this case, not engaging in 100% description mode while in the classroom observation puts the observer at peril for not providing the evidence teachers seek, need, and deserve.

Our confidence in the subject and grade level where we observe can affect the expectations we set for ourselves regarding the quality of feedback we can provide. A former math teacher, now principal, feels more comfortable providing feedback in a math classroom. Teachers of core areas can more easily transfer that confidence. This principal has grown to better understand language arts rooms, for example.

Areas where that confidence often still lags is in the performing and visual arts, career and technical areas, and foreign languages. In the five years of work in Decatur, Georgia, as I helped in building the proficiency of leaders to write high-quality feedback, I noted that written reflections from observers consistently asked the professional development planners to include more video clips and visits to art, music, physical education, and foreign language classrooms.

Description in those classrooms included the same actions and "more of" qualities delineated earlier:

- Quotations from teacher(s)
- Quotations from students
- Quantify whenever possible (e.g., tally)
- First letter of student names when known
- Times and durations

Table 3.13 Description: Level 1 Feedback

	1	2	3	4
Description *Purpose*: to see and hear what's going on in a classroom	Feedback is highly **descriptive**, balancing rich descriptions of student behaviors and teacher behaviors. Feedback includes **data** that was seen and heard, using direct **quotations** when appropriate. *"Three students put their heads down during the 10-minute movie. You remained at the back of the room speaking once to a student. It appeared that 10 students wrote something down. One student near the door used a Flow Map."*	Feedback is mostly **descriptive**, including **approximations** for what was seen and/or heard. Feedback may include student behaviors as well as teacher behaviors. *"Three students slept during the 10-minute movie. You remained at the back of the room watching the movie with the students."*	Feedback uses primarily **evaluative** and **interpretive** language. Feedback may include student behaviors as well as teacher behaviors. *"Students appeared off-task and bored during the movie despite your directions for them to take notes."*	Feedback primarily draws on **evaluative** language. Feedback is limited to teacher behaviors. *"You allowed the sleeping students too long before you intervened."*

It just may be certain actions here are heightened when the others seem impossible. In an instrumental music class, a performance-based discipline, it is not surprising when students speak less than the instructor. Their "speaking" is usually the performance on the instrument. The last item on the list above, "times and durations," becomes even more important in these instructional settings.

In a high school band classroom, I often use the stopwatch on my smartphone to collect durations of how long students play before being stopped by the teacher and which students get to play. I might construct a quick table like Table 3.14.

I might add another column to the chart below if I noticed a pattern like this in the teacher's speech: "Let's do it again." "One more time."

To be candid, as a former instrumental music teacher, I know the behavior of "Let's do it again" is an easy trap. I have that background knowledge and experience. However, I didn't have any meaningful feedback from my administrators to help me avoid the trap. I do remember a former principal falling asleep in the back of my band room as we rehearsed *Jupiter* by Holst. I accepted that as tacit feedback that the section clarinet's tone was quite sonorous and met the composer's expectations.

Experience as a teacher in each type of content is not needed— descriptive powers provide a leg up. If my former principal had simply tallied how often I used those deadly words, "Let's do it again," I could have accepted that data in a formative way and made a decision about my next steps.

In a foreign language classroom when the observer does not know the target language, it may not be worth the cognitive energy for the observer to attempt to write down what teachers and students are saying. Instead, "times and durations" can be quite advantageous to the receiver of the feedback, the teacher. Consider setting a stopwatch next to your computer

Table 3.14 Time Table in Performing Arts

Who	How long	Instruction provided before playing?
Clarinets	:35	Yes
Woodwinds	1:05	Yes
Low instruments	:20	No
Whole group	4:25	No

and click stop/start every time the target language is used. After you leave the classroom, engage in a bit of computation and construct a line like one of the following:

- 100% of the language spoken was in Spanish, and over 95% of the student talk was in the target language, too.
- Approximately 10–15% of instruction was in the target language.
- English was used 16 times in the observation, each time to translate what was just said in the target language.

I remember a visual arts teacher once lamenting to me that her administrator has tried to observe her several times but he consistently arrives after she has provided her opening instruction, so he leaves and tells her he will try again another time. Her complaint was not that he missed her opening; instead, she just wanted the observation to be done. She, like so many teachers, has never received feedback that provided a platform for her to engage in formative decisions about her practice.

As professional developers building observing skills in leaders, I have realized that many situations cause an administrator to leave the room, sending implicit messages to teachers that the next X number of minutes are not worthy of being observed:

- Students watching a movie/video
- Students silently reading
- Students taking a quiz/test
- Students engaging in individual practice

I find that performance-area teachers (e.g., visual and performing arts) are often masters at providing feedback, which would generally not be seen during a large-group mini-lesson.

I remember a specific co-observation with a career technical education assistant principal. We were in a fourth grade visual arts setting and as I grabbed the doorknob, he whispered, "I need you to know, I'm really nervous about this."

I smiled and responded, "Well, then this will be great learning for all three of us."

We observed 15 minutes of work time (yes—we missed the opening instruction!), and followed Ms. Dunbar around the room as she conferenced with students about their pencil drawings. We both wrote/ typed frenetically and left the room to check our inter-observer agreement, and then assign evaluative ratings for several domains.

As we chronologically reviewed our notes, it became apparent that Ms. Dunbar masterfully reminded students of the learning target through- out the observation. One hundred percent of her interactions with students included indications of how close they were to the target. As we offered that description on the teacher evaluation system form, along with three sample quotations from her student conferences, the assistant principal said to me, "That wasn't so bad. I thought being in career tech I wouldn't be able to do this. I believe I can."

Living in Description

Remember at the end of Chapter One quoting this Nathan Hale High School teacher in Seattle?

> I love when Ms. Donaldson [my assistant principal] comes to my room. She catches everything—what I'm doing, what the kids say, their reactions . . . it is so helpful. And I don't need to wait long for it, she sends it right away!

Rich, accurate description provides an equitable platform for each adult in our buildings to reflect on their actions and make decisions. In some ways, if we aren't doing this, we are sending an implicit message that the adults we support don't have the capacity to make sense of their own teaching decisions. This is not to say that individuals don't need coaches or conversations about practice. Written, descriptive feedback provides opportunities for educators to "autosupervise" (Zepeda, Wood, & O'Hair, 1996).

Darlene LeMaster, principal of an elementary school, remembers a very specific situation in which her descriptive skills were critical in pro- viding very meaningful feedback to a teacher about differentiation:

> A teacher was in a math workshop and was conferencing with individual students. In the past I may have sat back and watched the class. Now with description, I get up and listen in. She said

to one student: "Don't forget your number sentence." In another conference she said to another student, "Show your thinking in words, pictures, and numbers."

I had been having deep and repeated conversations with this teacher about differentiation. She claimed that she meets and exceeds the standard when she asks differentiated questions and provides differentiated scaffolds to students. When I wrote her this feedback, I simply added the student initials for these two students, for that was quite telling. The first student is academically stronger than the second and she chose to provide the stronger student very direct, very limiting feedback—contrary to what she voiced about her practices. My description to her was enough. Thank goodness I was building my prowess to describe really well. I finally have learned to "live in description."

Try It Yourself

1. Practice your descriptive skills during your next student lunch duty. Sit and write or type—not letting the pen leave the paper or your fingers hover over the computer keys. Set a timer for 60 seconds and just describe.

2. Choose the most reflective teacher on your faculty and tell him what you are trying to do. Spend 10 minutes in his room and work hard. Use the *Video Camera* (http://schoolreforminitiative. org/doc/video_camera.pdf) peer observation protocol to structure your debrief with the teacher. The purpose of this protocol is to build observational reliability between the observer and observed. Besides offering a gift to this respected colleague, you will receive feedback on your description!

3. The next time you debrief with a teacher, take the first 2–3 minutes for both of you to silently read the descriptive feedback. Consider starting with an iteration of this question: "What do you see in the description that aligns with what you remember about what happened when I was in your classroom?" Then the second question can be pursued: "What gaps might be there?"

4. If using protocols seems helpful for your practice, consider a Protocol Families organizing structure (http://schoolreforminitiative. org/doc/protocol_families.pdf): Read about some of the "Descriptive/Seeking Perspective" protocols referenced so far in this book (ATLAS Looking at Data, Collaborative Assessment Conference).

5. Try a "cold viewing" with all the leaders charged with observing in your building. Using it as diagnostic data, watch a short video or enter a classroom for no more than five minutes. Read each other's description aloud, verbatim, repeats intended. Use the T-chart structure found in Table 3.15 from Principal Kersey to create one for your team.

6. Test your descriptive powers out in a grade level or content that is less comfortable for you. Compare this narrative to a product from a content area or grade level that feels right at home.

7. In a meeting with adults (e.g., faculty, leadership, administrators), ask someone to collect descriptive data for you. Consider what 5–10 minutes of the meeting might be most helpful for you to have this chronicle. If you use any of the collected data in a formative way (e.g., to inform your decisions), make sure to tell the group why and how that descriptive data mattered.

8. Consider your learning from this chapter: What practices from this chapter are 10-degree changes? Which might require a 90-degree change in your practice? What might be first on your docket?

Table 3.15 Feedback Goal-Setting

What we want to do *more* of in our feedback	What we want to do *less* of in our feedback

Reference List

Bambrick-Santoyo, P. (2012). *Leverage leadership.* San Francisco, CA: Jossey-Bass.

Blythe, T., Allen, D., & Powell, B.S. (2008). *Looking together at student work* (2nd ed.). New York, NY: Teachers College Press.

Costa, A.L., Garmston, R.J., Ellison, J., & Hayes, C. (2014). *Cognitive coaching foundation seminars® learning guide* (10th ed.). Highlands Ranch, CO: Thinking Collaborative.

Darling-Hammond, L. (2013). *Getting teacher evaluation right.* New York, NY: Teachers College Press.

Gaines, E.J. (1983). *A Gathering of old men.* New York, NY: Random House.

Lawrence-Lightfoot. (1997). *The Art and science of portraiture.* San Francisco, CA: Jossey-Bass.

Popham, W.J. (2013). *Evaluating America's teachers: Mission possible?* Thousand Oaks, CA: Corwin.

TeachForAll. (2013, July 1). *A school that keeps learning—Part 3: Growth mindset* [Video file]. Retrieved from https://www.youtube.com/watch?v=DKM6QwQpe3g.

Wallace Foundation. (2015). *School leadership in action: Principal practices.* [video series].

Wiggins, G. (2012). Seven keys to effective feedback. *Educational Leadership, 70*(1), 10–16.

Zepeda, S.J., Wood, F., & O'Hair, M.J. (1996). A vision of supervision for 21st century schooling: Trends to promote change inquiry, and reflection. *Wingspan, 11*(2), 26–30.

Using Conditional Language to Ponder Change

4

Language matters. One word can be the difference between a teacher being open to an idea or not wanting to read another word. Like group facilitation, creating certain situations and interactions are helpful in causing group productivity and community. These facilitation moves can be learned. Similarly, educators who write feedback can learn the skill of using conditional language.

> As you walk in, the door creaks—loudly. It really doesn't matter because the volume level in the room supersedes any amount you could made by yourself. Tiptoeing carefully to avoid the paper, books, and art materials on the floor, you find a small kid-size chair and sit down. With an electronic tablet perched on your knees and eyes as large as saucers, you scan the room, searching for the teacher. The diminutive millennial's head pops up from underneath a kidney table with a book box for a guided reading group who appears to be listening to her. As Ms. Sullivan continues her learning target statement, she locks eyes with you for a moment, not missing a beat, and nods.

There seems to be quite a bit happening here. These seven- and eight-year-olds are excitedly engaged in literacy: talking, reading, and writing. Clearly Ms. Sullivan has set expectations about this time of day. She has successfully pulled a small group and the other students are also meaningfully tasked. Now, how to start writing her evaluation . . .

Chapter 3 laid the case for providing highly descriptive feedback for classroom teachers. This recounting of what was seen and heard in a classroom provides a rich repository from which teachers can truly learn, as they are the receivers and audience of our rigorous data collection. So, you're up for the challenge:

Six second graders are in an area called the Library Center, sitting with legs crossed debating vigorously about Junie B. Jones's motivation in a particular volume. Each student spoke during the interaction. Twice these words were used: "What's your evidence?" or a corollary: "How do you know?"

Two other students are writing at individual desks. When asked what they were learning, two of them responded similarly: "I'm learning to write an opinion piece that includes facts."

Eight other students engaged in partner reading at different places around the room. Each of them were sitting in EEKK style, as evidenced by a Daily Five anchor chart near the front of the room where a student had illustrated the elbow, elbow, knee, knee position.

A guided reading group of five students is at the back table, involved in a lesson with the following learning target posted on a small whiteboard: "I can identify a main idea using evidence from the text." During the 10-minute small group lesson, each student answered at least one question, read silently, and read aloud. When each student read aloud for less than one minute and anecdotal records were constructed, others continued to read silently.

Finally, four other students were involved in one or more of the following: walking around the room, picking up books and returning them to book boxes without opening them, and standing by partner readers until their classmates were asked to move.

After 10 minutes, a bell was rung and within two seconds, each student turned to look toward the sound. "This is your two-minute warning. We will engage in another Daily Five round later on. What was your job today?" It appeared that every student chanted in response: "Reading, writing, thinking!"

As the students bustled to line up for music class, you had taken advantage of their bold careens to slip out the door, not tiptoeing this time, probably stomping on a few pieces of authentic literacy on the floor.

You are delighted with the work of Ms. Sullivan, who clearly implements the important tenets of the school's literacy framework and wants to create highly functioning readers and writers. Quite proud of your descriptive powers, you now run stuck as you are concerned about the few disengaged students. You are fully supportive of Ms. Sullivan and want her to continue her hard work, so you will need to carefully frame this feedback.

Innovation Configuration Map

This desired outcome of **Conditional Language** on the Innovation Configuration Map in Table 4.1 includes descriptions of each variation as well as sample text. In this district's version of the High-Quality Innovation Configuration Map, the gray text indicates unacceptable variations (Levels 3 and 4).

Garmston and Wellman (2013) use the term "exploratory language" to describe this syntactical phenomenon. Observers better meet this desired outcome when they embrace the mindset of possibility using conditional and open language rather than definitive and closed phrasing.

Notice this attribute of high-quality feedback is not entitled "Suggestions." Instead, this desired outcome asks us to identify our use of

Table 4.1 Conditional Language Innovation Configuration Map

	1	2	3	4
Conditional language *Purpose:* to ponder a possible gap in practice	Conditional language is effectively used to help the reader **deeply consider gaps** or unintended results. "At least three standards in this observation seem to be affected by students' responsibilities when they arrive to class."	Conditional language is effectively used that would spur the reader to **pause and consider.** "It seems that there may be a connection between instructional time and classroom routines."	Conditional language is used to offer **suggestions.** "We are curious about the potential if students had a consistent routine every time they entered their room."	**Rhetorical questions** are used to suggest. "What might happen if you had something up on the interactive whiteboard the first moment students entered the room?"

conditional language. In keeping with the expressed intent for written feedback to be helpful for the receiver's *thinking,* the purpose of using conditional language is so the receiver can *ponder a possible gap in practice.* Even the purpose of conditional language has a conditional word in it: "possible." If we embrace the spirit of the synonym, "exploratory language" (Garmston & Wellman, 2013), we will use less definitive language when we really desire teachers to think deeply about the feedback we craft.

Using Questions

Table 4.2 Conditional Language: Level 4 Feedback

	1	2	3	4
Conditional language *Purpose:* to ponder a possible gap in practice				**Rhetorical questions** are used to suggest. *"What might happen if you had something up on the interactive whiteboard the first moment students entered the room?"*

Questions as Directives

If you have ever received meaningful feedback, it may have included questions written by the observer (e.g., Table 4.2). This practice is quite pervasive in feedback-construction but the intents and outcomes are rarely examined.

Written questions can fall on a continuum, using language developed by Glickman, Gordon, and Ross-Gordon (2013), found in Figure 4.1.

Figure 4.1 Supervisory Continuum

Adapted from Glickman et al. (2013).

Let's examine four questions offered to a teacher regarding student self-assessment:

- Could you have the students use a rubric?
- Do you think it might be advantageous if students used a rubric?
- What might happen if the students used a rubric?
- What do you need from me so students can assess their own work?

An observer may have written any or all of these from the nondirective side of the continuum, truly hoping the teacher, the receiver of this feedback, might entertain the idea of using a rubric. The communication gap occurs when the receiver, the teacher, reads the question in a directive way. The message received in that situation is the following: "You *should* have used a rubric."

Framing recommendations or requirements as questions is confusing. Children sometimes feign confusion when their parents use phrases like, "Should you clean your room now?" or "Could you do your homework before playing outside?" Children are generally not confused, and usually respond to these not-so-subtle pushes, completing the tasks the parent desires. Adults are another story.

Adults can feel manipulated by this practice. Consider this interaction at a high school:

> *An assistant principal is walking the halls between class change and notices that Mr. Hwong is not at his door. Peeking into the classroom, the administrator comments: "Hey, Mr. Hwong, can you do your hall duty?" Mr. Hwong rises from his computer, waves to the administrator, and mutters under his breath, "Of course, I can do it."*

This assistant principal attends some professional development about how to work more productively with adults and starts to change his tactic with teachers not fulfilling their duties:

"Miss Cabrera, good morning! What might happen out here if you did your hall duty?"

Adding nice conditional language to the question doesn't soften the blow—it actually can appear sarcastic.

This assistant principal has a choice to make—to be directive and clear about the requirement, or try and better understand the behavior. He chooses the latter:

"Ms. Olsen, I notice you aren't on your hall duty right now. What do you think are the possible impacts for our students when they don't see us in the halls?"

Certainly the question now requires some thinking, rather than just complying. However, the intent of the question is still the same: for the teacher to complete his/her hall duty. I contend that questions are never appropriate ways to communicate directives or requirements.

Another way to think about this difference is a theory from McGregor (1960). He identified supervisors driven by Theory X or Theory Y (Table 4.3).

In leadership preparation programs, this landmark theory is often used to encourage thoughtful discourse about micromanagement. In the context of teacher evaluation, it might serve as a decision-making lynchpin for an observer. Perhaps the question might be the following:

What evidence have I collected that description may not be enough? What else do I know that would better inform this decision?

Table 4.3 Theory X and Y Supervisors

Theory X supervisors	Theory Y supervisors
Believe people are incapable of working autonomously	Believe people are capable of self-direction in analyzing their learning and professional development

Source: © Routledge 2012, Sally J. Zepeda, *Instructional Supervision: Applying Tools and Concepts.* Used with permission.

Questions as Suggestions

All of the aforementioned examples seem to have a clear compliance purpose. However, other times questions may be used to offer a true suggestion for classroom practice. In fact, sometimes principals require their assistant principals to include suggestions in their feedback. A tacit belief present in this practice is that teachers need more ideas. After all, why did websites like Teachers Pay Teachers or Pinterest launch in the first place?

When slowed down, the thinking process of adults when they receive this sort of feedback is not productive. Consider the representative think-aloud in Table 4.4 from a kindergarten teacher after reading her feedback.

The following assumptions may be underlying these few simple statements:

- By posing a change in something she has already tried, she feels defeated and frustrated.
- The teacher believes her job is to please her evaluator.

An important outcome of written feedback is that the reader, the teacher, *thinks.* Sometimes school leaders want to use written feedback as an opportunity for the receiving teacher to *learn.* Learning is not the same as thinking.

Consider the words from my wife (a teacher) after attending a summer professional development day focused on technology.

Me: "How was your PD today?"
Her: "I learned a ton. Check out all these notes."
Me: "So now what are you thinking?"
Her: [pause] "I didn't *think* about anything. I guess I got app-ed."

Table 4.4 Think Aloud From a Teacher Receiving Feedback

Written Feedback	Think-Aloud
What might happen if your students sat in a different formation during the read-aloud?	*I've tried this before. This is my third seating chart since the quarter began. I don't know what else he wants.*

The joy of using the word "app" as a verb rather than a noun associated with tablet applications certainly made us laugh. However, this situation also demonstrates the power of *thinking* opposed to *learning*. Several months later, it is highly probable that this list of tablet apps will still be just that—a list. If she had deeply thought about one or two apps, it is more probable the professional development had some residue, some evidence the day impacted her teaching practice.

Questions as Reflection-Provoking

A greater percentage of school leaders have now been trained in coaching strategies. Some of the first wave of instructional coaches have transitioned into administration. These very well-intended leaders probably know a thing or two about questioning. They might be able to use closed and open questions with facility, or even frame deeply probing questions that cause a shift in perspective. However, these interactions are best held in person, not through written feedback.

Teachers are placed in an untenable position when faced with questions in written feedback. Their internal dialogue might go like this:

Am I supposed to write back?
Do I need to write back?
If I write back, where and how do I do that? Through email? Through the teacher evaluation portal? What does that look like? Is there a

Table 4.5 Level 4 Feedback and Something Better

Level 4 Feedback	Better Iteration
Do you think it might be productive if students used a rubric?	Perhaps the students would have been more clear on the assignment with a rubric.
What might happen if your students sat in a different formation during the read aloud?	I wonder what a different formation might do for students' attention spans.

preferred or "right" format? Will what I write go in my file? Is there really a file? Who has it?

Maybe I shouldn't write back—perhaps my supervisor wants a conference with me in person to discuss all these questions. Do I schedule it or just pop in?

Read Table 4.5 and consider some of the questions already posed in this chapter, transformed from Level 4 feedback to something slightly better.

Innovation Configuration Map

Level 3 feedback, as described in Table 4.6, does not use questions to disguise a recommendation. Conditional language is used to frame the suggestion; however, the suggestion isn't really a suggestion.

Look back at Table 4.5 and ask yourself: Does this better iteration really make the feedback much better?

Table 4.6 Conditional Language: Level 3 Feedback

	1	2	3	4
Conditional language *Purpose:* to ponder a possible gap in practice			Conditional language is used to offer **suggestions.** *"We are curious about the potential if students had a consistent routine every time they entered their room."*	**Rhetorical questions** are used to suggest. *"What might happen if you had something up on the interactive whiteboard the first moment students entered the room?"*

Suggestions

After the "Try It Yourself" activities at the end of Chapter 3, you might be questioning other habits evidenced by your written feedback, particularly the practice of suggesting. If we are truly in descriptive mode 100% of the time while in a classroom and work toward 80% of the final product remaining descriptive, how might suggestions be added? Before we talk specifically about that practice, it may be helpful to identify your own behaviors.

How Often and to Whom?

I suspect you are not currently aware of how often you give suggestions and who the beneficiaries of these little nuggets are. You might write one concrete suggestion to a third grade teacher, then offer a plethora of suggestions to someone else. If you stopped to tease out that practice, I suspect you would find patterns.

Observers tend to offer multiple suggestions when one or more of the following factors is present:

- the observer has teaching experience in the content being observed,
- the observer has teaching experience in the grade level being observed,
- the teacher is new to the profession,
- the teacher is new to the teaching assignment (i.e., grade level, content), or
- the teacher is in crisis.

This all seems perfectly logical: we speak fluently (and often frequently) about things in which we have expertise. It gives us confidence and buttresses us through the observations where we feel less competent. For principals in primary and elementary schools, the observations we dread may be in the special areas, activities, or electives: art, music, physical education, or foreign language. In secondary schools, a principal who taught in the humanities may take a deep breath before entering AP physics, or an assistant principal who is a recovering math expert may feel some angst as she turns the knob in the agricultural science lab.

The problem with this perfectly logical and commonplace practice is that it is inequitable. If the quality of the feedback received depends on the subject matter expertise or deep pedagogical knowledge of the observer, we have created some departments or grade levels that are marginalized, and others perhaps that are overly attended.

In addition to subject or grade level expertise, an assumption about novice teachers often silently affects a leader's proclivity to craft multiple suggestions. Although the context for teaching and learning has changed dramatically over the past 20 years, schools still tend to treat novice teachers as an endangered species. Many schools have entirely scripted professional development programs tailored to these teachers, complete with monthly topics deemed relevant for them, despite some research that indicates novice teachers' needs are quite different from these topical experiences (Van Soelen, 2003). For some, the content is just right but for others it is far from the mark.

Context has changed in three ways:

1. Teachers new to the profession are no longer 22-year-old white women fresh out of college. First-year teachers can now be alternatively certified, mid-career changers, former paraprofessionals, or in the process of completing coursework as they also teach their first group of students.

2. Twenty years ago, a teacher with a deep set of varying strategies emerged from possibly teaching multiple grades, enrolling in graduate school, completing summer professional development, or consistently meeting with other teachers to talk shop. Now, a simple Google search yields millions of hits ranging from a first grade teacher's blog of her attempt at a writer's workshop to a scholarly article with the results of a randomized trial. There is no longer an earning of stripes through years of service in order to be strategy-rich and experience-informed.

3. Although all teachers new to the profession are not in their twenties, those that are in that age group enter teaching with different markings. This generation seeks feedback, perhaps craves it. However, they are not desirous of feedback that is consistently directive. Instead they seek options, and would prefer to create their own if possible. This generation frequently applied what they were learning in their own K–12 schooling, so it seems perfectly logical to continue that pattern into adulthood.

It is time to introduce the final factor in deciding whether or not to give suggestions: your own feedback stories. An observer's teaching history matters, as does the experience level of the teacher receiving the feedback. However, it may be our own feedback stories that matter the most.

Although I do not know of a research study to validate this claim, it meets the logic test: each school leader was viewed by someone at some point as an effective teacher. Whether or not the criteria used to determine effectiveness were consistent or valid, research-based or even explicit, it is irrelevant for this argument. Highly effective teachers (as perceived by some other person) receive less feedback.

When I ask school leaders the questions listed in "Try It Yourself" at the end of this chapter, some are quite stumped. They have never contemplated their feedback dearth as hugely impacting *a,* if not *the,* primary function of their current job.

Why this fact matters is that our school leaders are being asked to write highly descriptive and highly usable feedback when they have never received any. This argument is similar to differentiation: we have asked an entire profession of teachers to differentiate when the vast majority has never had their personal learning differentiated.

What happens with differentiation is due to this knowing/experience gap, and the term differentiation is broadly applied—and frequently misapplied—to a whole host of practices. Teachers have interpreted differentiation how they wish because schools and school systems often do not define it.

What often happens is school leaders make an assumption regarding feedback because no one has defined feedback cogently for or with them:

highly usable = suggestions

Because school leaders want to be helpful—it is not their desire to write highly unusable or wasteful feedback—they spend their feedback energy on the bottom 10% of their teaching staff. These narratives are often loaded with suggestions and resources.

Conversely, these observers perpetuate the pattern they experienced when they were in the classroom. They assume that highly effective teachers do not need suggestions; therefore, their feedback is not highly usable:

highly usable ≠ suggestions

Highly effective teachers receive something like the following:

- Observations using only the quantitative rubric digits (often the highest rating)
- Observations relying on the language of the rubrics as narrative feedback (oftentimes copying the language verbatim)
- Observations replete with kudos and "attaboys"

When each of the practices in this book are practiced and consistently applied, a culture of feedback (Van Soelen, 2013) is created where evaluations are not viewed as positive strokes. Instead each teacher has an equitable chance of becoming consciously competent: using their observational data to make better decisions for their students.

How?

We are affected by our own teaching histories and the assumptions we might hold about teachers new to the profession. We also may have dealt with our desire to overcompensate because of our feedback stories.

Even with these in proper perspective, once we have decided to offer a suggestion, at times it feels clumsy. Consider the four questions stated earlier about self-assessment, with some other statements added:

- Could you have the students use a rubric?
- Do you think it might be advantageous if students used a rubric?
- What might happen if the students used a rubric?
- I wonder what might happen if the students were to use a rubric.
- Self-assessment is a teaching strategy that would be helpful.
- I'm excited about the potential of students assessing their own work.
- What help would you need from me so students can assess their own work?

Some of these statements use conditional language. Table 4.7 offers some examples of conditional words, displayed in two categories.

The text in the first column of Table 4.7, "Related to Ideas," is worthy of consideration by leaders writing observational feedback. These words can be effectively used to frame suggestions without using rhetorical questions.

Table 4.7 Conditional Words

Related to Ideas	Related to Time/Quantity
could	some
might	almost
wonder	many
appears	most
perhaps	likely
seem	typically
consider	usually
possible	frequently
may	

Table 4.8 Transforming Suggestions With Conditional Language

Original Suggestion	Reframed Using Conditional Language
Try using some of the new National Geographic guided reading book sets we just purchased.	The new National Geographic guided reading book sets **may be** helpful in this unit.
Be clear with students when they are not meeting your expectations.	Two times the success criteria for "working independently time" were referenced, other times not. Consider how the consistent use of these criteria **might** make the situation more pleasing for adults and students.

Ponder the transformations in Table 4.8, particularly those marked with **boldface** type.

However, conditional language is not magical in its use. It does not automatically produce the conditions for the reader of the feedback, the teacher, to ponder a possible gap in practice.

Conditional language can only be effective if the intent is truly conditional. In other words, if a leader needs or will require a change to take place, then conditional language is not effective.

"Perhaps you should post the learning intentions for all students to see."

If this is a schoolwide expectation or agreement, then the word *perhaps* makes the situation unclear to the receiver—like there is a condition she/he needs to ponder.

Reframed:

"Remember our schoolwide expectation where learning intentions are consistently posted for each student to see."

Perhaps the decision of whether to use conditional language or not could also be envisioned on a continuum, inspired by McGregor, as demonstrated in Figure 4.2.

So the question might be the following:

What sort of conditional language might I use to encourage the receiver to truly ponder this feedback? Am I really suggesting at all?

I chose to not use conditional language in the two examples below. Using directive language, these aren't suggestions. I didn't want to cause misunderstanding:

Example 1: "It is imperative that each adult in Hallway B is at their door between class changes."

Example 2: "The alphabet song that was used has several mispronounced phonemes, for instance, [d] is pronounced [duh]. As you choose a different song to use, please ensure all sounds are correctly modeled."

Figure 4.2 Using Theory X and Y to Make Decisions

Level 2 Feedback

Table 4.9 Conditional Language: Level 2 Feedback

	1	2	3	4
Conditional language Purpose: to ponder a possible gap in practice		Conditional language is effectively used that would spur the reader to **pause and consider.** "It seems that there may be a connection between instructional time and classroom routines."	Conditional language is used to offer **suggestions.** "We are curious about the potential if students had a consistent routine every time they entered their room."	**Rhetorical questions** are used to suggest. "What might happen if you had something up on the interactive whiteboard the first moment students entered the room?"

Using Conditional Language to Frame Ideas

So, you believe you have ridded your written feedback of directives disguised as questions (Level 4 in Table 4.9). You have some thinking you would like to spur but don't want to just offer directives framed with conditional language (Level 3 in Table 4.9).

Conditional language helps the receivers, the teachers, to accept the feedback and deeply consider it—to really *think* about it. When observers write with definitive tone and authoritative language, the purpose changes: it is no longer about thinking, it is about *implementing*.

There is a time and place to write very specific steps and requirements in a teacher evaluation narrative. However, not only are they infrequent, those times are also prefaced by multiple other observations that would frame possible gaps in teaching practice through the use of conditional language, allowing the teacher to ponder that gap and act on his/her thinking.

For instance, in a middle school working on improving the quality and use of learning intentions (Wiliam, 2011), the **first** piece of feedback might sound like this:

> It is clear that students were involved in their work, as each of the 24 sixth graders were performing mathematics calculations. The learning intention was posted on the whiteboard: "Understand the concept of a unit rate a/b associated with a ratio $a:b$ with $b \neq 0$."
>
> When asked what they were learning today, two students similarly responded: "working on ratios."

A **second** observation might determine that the gap regarding learning intentions is still present in the classroom:

> Students were working in groups, ranging from three to five students each. Each group was solving a set of problems with negative and positive numbers, indicating a partial match to the learning intention: "I can understand that positive and negative numbers are used together to describe quantities having opposite directions or values."
>
> The "I can" statement allows students to own their learning and assess their progress. When asked, students knew "tricks" or "cheats" to solve equations with negative and positive numbers, but were not able to explain the importance of the learning intention. Consider how you might include something in the assessment that requires students to explain their understanding of the learning intention.

And possibly a **third** observation still does not yield the change the observer desires:

> Four stations are set up for students as they work toward the learning intention: "I can correctly explain absolute value." Three of the learning stations include independent work while one station worked in a small group with support. During independent stations, students consistently worked, never needing reminders about behavior or focus.

The work of each station was algorithmic in that students applied memorized steps to correctly solve the problems. In comparing the station work with the standard, a gap exists: explaining. In planning learning experiences, use the verb in the standard as a litmus test. This verb should be demonstrated by each student during instruction ("We do") and in an assessment ("You do") that is used in a formative way.

This teacher exemplifies some important structures (e.g., group work, stations), and evidence exists that she is working hard in planning for her students. However, each observation demonstrates a deficit in the area of learning intentions. Armed with clear, concrete description, the suggestions range from nondirective (first) to directive (third).

Other examples might include the following—all of these would include rich description (as the walls) to ground these interpretive statements (the roof):

- *By using graphic organizers and sentence frames for each writing assignment, consider if any students might be ready for that scaffold to be removed.*
- *Based on the students' questions, perhaps they need an activity where they actively experience what that historical time must have been like (e.g., simulation).*
- *It may be confusing for students to apply a visual cue to this biological task that is intended to be criteria-based.*

Or this one, offered with a bit more context:

As questions were asked during the lesson, sometimes students were called on individually; other times unison response was used. When unison response was used and a question was asked immediately after the student responses, students would respond with the other answer:

T: "Is this a plant or an animal?"
many S: "Plant!"
T: "How do you know it was a plant?"
many S: "Animal!"

One way that might avoid this flip-flopping is to preface the second question with a direction:
"I just want to hear from individual students here: How do you know?"

Putting It All Together

Reconsidering the inclusion of questions into written feedback and being clear about whether or not to use conditional language is at the heart of the complete desired outcome of conditional language. Rich description is provided and only then does conditional language, carefully chosen, pivot us into an interpretive part of the conversation, reserving at least 80% of our narrative to ground our interpretations.

Levels 1 and 2 in this desired outcome of conditional language are closely connected. Both of them are acceptable iterations, as neither of them is shaded. Both of them contain examples of conditional language. Neither of them embed disguised recommendations.

Table 4.10 Desired Outcome: Conditional Language on the High-Quality Feedback Innovation Configuration Map

	1	2	3	4
Conditional language *Purpose:* to ponder a possible gap in practice	Conditional language is effectively used to help the reader **deeply consider gaps** or unintended results. *"At least three standards in this observation seem to be affected by students' responsibilities when they arrive to class."*	Conditional language is effectively used that would spur the reader to **pause and consider.** *"It seems that there may be a connection between instructional time and classroom routines."*	Conditional language is used to offer **suggestions.** *"We are curious about the potential if students had a consistent routine every time they entered their room."*	**Rhetorical questions** are used to suggest. *"What might happen if you had something up on the interactive whiteboard the first moment students entered the room?"*

Remember Ms. Sullivan and her reading workshop? Perhaps the entire narrative with Level 1 feedback for description and Level 1 feedback for conditional language could look something like this:

Six second graders are in an area called the Library Center, sitting with legs crossed debating vigorously about Junie B. Jones's motivation in a particular volume. Each student spoke during the interaction. Twice these words were used: "What's your evidence?" or a corollary: "How do you know?"

Two other students are writing at individual desks. When asked what they were learning, two of them responded similarly: "I'm learning to write an opinion piece that includes facts."

Eight other students engaged in partner reading at different places around the room. Each of them were sitting in EEKK style, as evidenced by a Daily Five anchor chart near the front of the room where a student had illustrated the elbow, elbow, knee, knee position.

A guided reading group of five students is at the back table, involved in a lesson with the following learning target posted on a small whiteboard: "I can identify a main idea using evidence from the text." During the 10-minute small group lesson, each student answered at least one question, read silently and read aloud. When each student read aloud for less than one minute and anecdotal records were constructed, others continued to read silently.

Finally, four other students were involved in one or more of the following: walking around the room, picking up books and returning them to book boxes without opening them, and standing by partner readers until they were asked to move. This workshop engaged 84% of the students in important, meaningful literacy experiences. It appears there are implications for each student in this workshop when 100% of students are not reading, writing, and thinking.

After 10 minutes, a bell was rung and within two seconds, each student turned to look toward the sound. "This is your two-minute warning. We will engage in literacy time again later on today. What was your job today?" It appeared that every student chanted: "Reading, writing, thinking!"

After a hearty dose of description, only two sentences of interpretation (clearly indicated through the use of underlining in the feedback above) are needed for Ms. Sullivan to ponder this gap in practice. Because she is a thoughtful practitioner, moving toward autosupervision, this narrative is exactly what she needs to improve.

Try It Yourself

1. Review three observations from a grade level or subject area in which you never taught. Then perform a similar review for subject matter or learner ages where you are quite confident. Where did you offer more suggestions? What issues of equity arise when you consider what you learned in this chapter about conditional language? Which teachers are you causing more *thinking* with and less *learning* with?

2. Use a *Microlabs* (http://schoolreforminitiative.org/doc/microlabs.pdf) protocol with others or try these questions with just yourself:

   a. When you think about feedback as a learner, talk about a time when feedback propelled you forward. Who offered it, what form did it take, how did you use it?

   b. What might be the very best things that would happen if each teacher in our buildings consistently received highly descriptive, highly usable feedback?

   c. If the implementation of our teacher evaluation process was on a continuum from "logistical process to be checked off" to "used as a school and teacher improvement strategy," where do we currently fall on that continuum and what evidence do you see or hear to support that assertion?

3. In your own practice, reconsider your frequency of using reflective questions. Cognitive coaching theorists (Costa & Garmston, 2002)

posit the power of paraphrasing. After studying different types of paraphrases (e.g., acknowledge and clarify, summarize and organize, shift for abstraction) for differing purposes, try an observation post-conference completely using paraphrases rather than questions.

4. Protocol Families Connection (http://schoolreforminitiative.org/doc/protocol_families.pdf): Read about some of the "Refining" protocols, considering how you might use a refining process to create feedback documents that more closely align with your expectations or the High-Quality Feedback Innovation Configuration Map.

5. Find an observation where you wrote several suggestions. Work either independently with others to rewrite using conditional language.

6. Consider your learning from this chapter: What practices from this chapter are 10-degree changes? Which might require a 90-degree change in your practice? What might be first on your docket?

Reference List

Costa, A.L., & Garmston, R.J. (2002). *Cognitive coaching: A foundation for renaissance schools.* Norwood, MA: Christopher-Gordon.

Garmston, R.J., & Wellman, B.M. (2013). *The adaptive school: A sourcebook for developing collaborative groups.* Ranham, MD: Rowman & Littlefield.

Glickman, C.D., Gordon, S.P., & Ross-Gordon, J.M. (2013). *SuperVision and instructional leadership: A developmental approach* (9th ed.). New York, NY: Pearson.

McGregor, D. (1960). *The human side of enterprise.* New York, NY: McGraw-Hill.

Van Soelen, T.M. (2003). *If Polly had been there: An uncommon journey toward teacher development and induction* (Unpublished doctoral dissertation). University of Georgia, Athens, GA.

Van Soelen, T.M. (2013). Building a sustainable culture of feedback. *Performance Improvement Journal, 52*(4), 22–29.

Wiliam, D. (2011). *Embedded formative assessment.* Bloomington, IN: Solution Tree.

5

Why Point of View Is Significant

Language matters. Sometimes writing the narrative portions of our teacher evaluation feedback seems clumsy. As school leaders, we can sometimes craft a beautiful email or an inviting parent letter but can't quite make that leap for teacher evaluations. These products sometimes sound quite clinical:

The teacher purposefully moved around the room, checking for understanding (Marzano, A for L, UbD, DI). Rigorous, research-based interventions have been put in place for students in Tier III who have not met progress monitoring benchmarks.

On the other hand, perhaps our motivational, celebratory side may get the best of us as we observe something exciting:

I just love the way your students responded to the hook!!! I was at the planning session where your life science team developed the scenario. I know that everyone was not "on board" with the idea, but you certainly now have something to share with them! Way to go!

Although the previous skills of description and conditional language would help ameliorate a few of the gaps present in the previous two examples, the examples represent another change that is the subject of this chapter: inconsistent point of view. We can't quite decide which sounds better: "Mrs. Lancaster spread out . . ." "She spread out . . ." "You spread out . . ." "I noticed that you spread out . . ." This chapter articulates what teachers want it to sound like so they can truly process and accept the feedback.

In Decatur, Georgia, point of view mattered immensely, particularly with the concurrent implementation of a new teacher evaluation system that caused varying degrees of consternation. Here's what Kendria, a pre-kindergarten teacher reflected:

> I just enjoy it [the observations and feedback] because I'm starting to grow professionally, and it's helping the students. What I'm hearing from the students and the parents has been wonderful this year. It's been a great experience—it was tough in the beginning. I was a little hurt! But once I really took myself out of it and looked at it objectively, I was able to learn so much. And I'm excited—it just started. I can't wait to see how I continue to grow.

"Took myself out of it"—that is a reflective practitioner! Kendria was able to successfully negotiate the changes her observers had made in how to give feedback. After Kendria had been teaching for a decade (and receiving anecdotal positive parent and school leader reviews), a substantial change was occurring in her district: reconfiguration.

This district reconfiguration was more than a redistricting. It included changing the school grade spans. Previous PK–5 schools were now transitioned to either K–3 or 4–5. All district pre-kindergarten classes were grouped together in one facility. Formerly a "singleton" teacher (like a single AP music theory course is called a singleton in high school scheduling) in previous schools, now birds of a feather were being asked to flock together. Collaboration was not only logistically possible but required. With these pre-kindergarten teachers, over the next few years, a new curriculum was launched, new assessments were implemented, instructional coaching supported classroom teachers, and a new teacher evaluation system was launched.

Kendria's observers worked diligently to undo some of their own previous behaviors as observers: listing multiple strategies to try, summarizing large blocks of time, and focusing on the adults. Now feedback was steeped in description. Ideas were thoughtfully crafted using conditional language. And, most relevant to this chapter, point of view was consistent.

"Took myself out of it" was made possible in part when her observers chose the point of view that gave her the permission and the space to do so.

Education Is Unique

Performance reviews in other professions rarely include specific reports based on single observations. Observation certainly is an important part of most performance reviews: a shift manager at McDonald's watches the crew while also participating in the work; an accounting supervisor may occasionally sit in on a client meeting with a junior CPA. However, the very act of creating a document that specifically details those observations is quite education-specific. Imagine if a salesperson received a transcript of his last client meeting, courtesy of his supervisor who was on the call with him. Consider a dental hygienist receiving a written play-by-play of how well she chose and distributed the necessary instruments during a tooth removal.

Looking to other occupations and their performance review practices does not help educational leaders write better observational feedback. Performance improvement specialists primarily focus on the delivery of the feedback: how to have a crucial conversation, a difficult conversation, a challenging conversation, a fierce conversation, a hard conversation, or just a regular-old conversation. An element in these conversations is almost always specificity. However, rarely would any of these business consultants encourage an employer to observe and document an employee so the employee can read and make sense of what was collected.

This lack of professional development for educational leaders in how to write high-quality feedback is clearly exhibited in the following samples. Remembering the large high school with 23 observers from Chapter 3: watch this three-minute video clip and "write everything you saw and heard."

In reading through a sampling of the responses in Table 5.1, this time note the inconsistent point of view:

"Jon"
"He"
"Man"
"The teacher"
"Your"
"I"

Clearly these observers have not built shared understanding about what point of view to use in their writing.

Table 5.1 Response Samples Attempting Description

As Jon came running into the room, the students were writing. He was talking about voting and slavery. He showed them how he would be in the room, and the slaves would be out in the hall. He moved around the room as he talked throughout the lesson. He asked numerous questions and got some feedback from the students. At this point, the students stopped writing and listened to him.
Man physically ran into the room, talking and describing anti-slavery people. Then he referenced John Brown African American Leader gentleman Leader on the screen. Walked around the room talking moving around to certain students.
Teacher is very illustrative to get to the points of learning to students. Asked open-ended questions about topic being covered. Teacher active and animated in classroom in describing slavery.
Your energy and enthusiasm for the lesson (slavery) kept the students engaged.
I noticed several students not taking notes during class. Are you worried about them? I think the paraprofessional could take a more active role with those students.

Even an individual may have difficulty with consistency. This sample from a school leader shifts point of view multiple times during the narrative:

You did not provide me with a lesson plan for today's lesson either by email or through being uploaded to the platform. I did not see any standards, essential question, or KUD posted. Neither you nor the students explicitly referenced any standards or learning targets. The class period ended while I was in the room; the teacher did not summarize any learning goals for the day with students. After the bell rang, Ms. Clarke reminded students to bring their homework.

Choosing a particular point of view or vacillating between various points of view might be an unconscious phenomenon; school leaders never giving the habit much thought. In combination with descriptive and conditional language, this chapter ensures that the leader will make a structural decision about writing that invites the reader, the teacher, to read the feedback and accept it as being more about practice than the person.

Innovation Configuration Map

The desired outcome of **Point of View** has only three iterations: the ideal (Level 1) and two other possibilities. The desired outcome creates narratives teachers can more readily accept as they temporarily distance themselves from the observation.

Table 5.2 Point of View Innovation Configuration Map

	1	2	3	4
Point of View *Purpose:* to accept the feedback more about practice than the person	Feedback primarily focuses on **actions** instead of the teacher. Passive voice pervades the feedback. *"The ACTIVBoard was used to model the Circle Map."*	Feedback is primarily written focusing on the **observer.** *"I observed that the ACTIVBoard was used to model the Circle Map."*	Feedback is primarily written from **another** **person's** point of view. *"You used the ACTIVBoard to model the Circle Map."* *"The teacher used the ACTIVBoard to model the Circle Map."* *"Ms. Smith used the ACTIVBoard to model the Circle Map."*	

Level 3 Feedback

Table 5.3 indicates the point of view which places feedback as Level 3. The Level 3 feedback example found in Table 5.4 is only part of a formative evaluation a teacher received. In the narrative's totality, "you," "your," or "you're" is used 82 times. Although each use of second person is either to praise the teacher or describe something, the second person takes its toll. Imagine a finger pointed at you 82 times.

There is also something important to note here about the use of description. The better iteration version uses description as the main event, not an appetizer. Sometimes observers are proficient in describing what

Table 5.3 Point of View: Level 3 Feedback

	1	2	3	4
Point of View *Purpose:* to accept the feedback more about practice than the person			Feedback is primarily written from **another person's** point of view. *"**You** used the ACTIVBoard to model the Circle Map."* *"**The teacher** used the ACTIVBoard to model the Circle Map."* *"**Ms. Smith** used the ACTIVBoard to model the Circle Map."*	

they see and hear, but venture into the E of DIE, evaluation, when they try to expound on the description. Here is a partial list of the evaluative language used in the Level 3 feedback:

- I love
- Obviously comfortable
- Enjoy their time
- I like
- Positive (twice)

So, another reason to be conscious about point of view is the goal of 80% description.

Movement

Cognitive coaching theorists (Costa & Garmston, 2002) use a goal of "movement" in their conversations: "How has this conversation helped

Table 5.4 Level 3 Feedback and Something Better

Level 3 Feedback	Better Iteration
I love how your kids respond to you. They tell you jokes, hinge on every word, and participate fully as you review for the day. They are obviously comfortable with you and trust you enough to share answers, talk about academic connections between your class and their world, and to laugh and enjoy their time. There are really no disruptions for you to attend to, but when kids are reviewing, to get them back to attention, you simply click a clicker, and all kids are back on task. No need to raise your voice. This indicates that you've reviewed expectations with your kids and have re-visited and reinforced them as necessary. I like how, even in the lab, you are able to create an inviting learning environment for them. You do this today by sitting them around you (almost like an elementary school's "Carpet Time") and speaking to them in a positive, hushed tone. You've arranged the materials for today (Vegemite) to help ensure a positive, efficient experience.	The students participate fully as they seem to be in rapt attention to jokes and other enticing moves. They are obviously comfortable and trustful, expecting the following: share answers, talk about academic connections to the world, and laugh and enjoy. Disruptions are minimal to none. Expectations have been set and monitored as evidenced by the clicker that is used to gain their attention as they are reviewing. An inviting learning environment was created in the computer lab using space ("Carpet Time") and a quiet voice. The materials (Vegemite) were arranged in a way to ensure an efficient taste test.

you move your thinking?" Coaches talented in these interactions have mastered several frameworks and specific skills. Among these very specific abilities is a focus on the coachee. Cognitive coaches concentrate on keeping a "spotlight" on their coachee. Don't imagine a hot Broadway theater spotlight, nor a single incandescent bulb in a darkened FBI interrogation room. Instead, picture the coachee with light coming straight from above, casting a circular glow around him or her.

This focused light affects the coach's choice of language during the coaching session. Since the light is on the coachee, all language spoken should benefit the coachee's thinking. Any mention of anything else breaks the coachee's thinking and that re-focus takes precious time to re-construct.

Read the following example and ponder the three possible coach responses:

Coachee: "I have been having trouble with the Biology PLC. They are always late for our Tuesday sessions and several of them come in with nothing in their hand—not even a piece of paper or a pen. I think they are relying on me to do all the work for them, both the pre-work and the work after the meeting. Frankly, I'm not getting anything out of the meeting, except grief, that is."

Response A:
Coach: "I'm upset about how they are treating you. They really should not be doing that."

Response B:
Coach: "What I'm hearing you say is that your colleagues are always late to collaboration."

Response C:
Coach: "You are frustrated that your colleagues find this meeting a waste of time."

Although the content of each response is slightly different and those responses could provoke some quality discussion, the key learning for this chapter about point of view is the pronoun use.

Response A: *I*
Response B: *I*
Response C: *You*

Keeping a consistent light on the coachee's thinking requires a coach to eliminate any reference to him/herself. Gone are these words: *I, me, my, myself, mine.*

It takes discipline to re-tool your speech patterns and learn something new. Students and adults who code switch learn these skills and hone them through practice.

Level 2 Feedback

Many current principals have experienced a communication tool that emerged in the 1970s: "I-messages." If a principal is over the age of 50,

Table 5.5 Point of View: Level 2 Feedback

	1	2	3	4
Point of View *Purpose:* to accept the feedback more about practice than the person		Feedback is primarily written focusing on the **observer.** *"**I** observed that the ACTIVBoard was used to model the Circle Map."*	Feedback is primarily written from **another person's** point of view. *"**You** used the ACTIVBoard to model the Circle Map."* *"**The teacher** used the ACTIVBoard to model the Circle Map."* *"**Ms. Smith** used the ACTIVBoard to model the Circle Map."*	

Table 5.6 Level 2 Feedback and Something Better

Level 2 Feedback	Better Iteration
I know when I came in you told me that students were working in many different places. I think that it is great that you can structure your classroom for a time when so many different activities are going on with your students and they have the chance to all be caught up.	Students were working in many different places. The classroom was successfully structured with multiple activities occurring at the same time.

they may have learned about how to use I-messages in their preparation programs:

When someone is consistently late for work, use an I-message: "When you are late for work, I am worried about you."

Principals aged 35–50 may have experienced I-messages from the other end—adults using I-messages on them:

Son, when you are late for curfew, I am worried about you. [And the self-talk in the father's head: *And I'm going to wring your neck!*]

Younger principals may only know about I-messages from sitcoms or reality TV that mocks this practice. For readers in this bracket, search for episodes of *That '70s Show* for numerous examples.

Although I-messages may have been developed with the best of intentions, their use has extended to teacher evaluation practices (Tables 5.5 and 5.6). This behavior does not align with the "spotlight" image from cognitive coaching.

As cognitive coaches consistently speak in second-person point of view, they are über-focused on listening—and a particular kind of listening, at that. To build their capacity of listening to understand, four listening setasides are learned so these coaches can listen with enough savvy to provide a response that moves the coachee's thinking.

Listening Setasides

Instead of listening to understand, sometimes we *listen to solve problems.* Consider this school leader:

> *James is really great at solving problems. In fact, he's awesome at it. He prides himself on solving issues before anyone calls the district office. Frankly, he may never have been promoted after only being an assistant principal for one year if he wasn't good at problem-solving. Some people hate the, "Do you have a minute?" James loves it! When someone calls his name down the long school hallway, I think he gets a little tingly with excitement. Sometimes people don't have a problem when they come talk to him, but by the time they leave him, they have had a problem and he solved it!*

Perhaps you were laughing as you read that previous paragraph. It may have been the nervous laughter of self-identification.

As our colleagues or family members are speaking, sometimes you may realize that you are *listening to tell stories*. Consider this experienced department chair:

> *Doris has been around the block. Since she has the longest attendance streak in this district, she's seen a lot. In fact, she taught the principal when he was in high school. What a goofy kid he was. I remember Doris telling a story about when he. . . . Man, Doris just sucks me in with her stories! They are so good and she tells them so well. When others talk to Doris, she seems to take a brief hiatus after a few sentences. She listens enough to get the gist and then opens a mental Rolodex. It only takes a few seconds for her to cull though her experiences and pull out a story that really helps the other person. Kids and adults alike tell her she is such a great storyteller.*

If you are a storyteller, you may have read the paragraph up to "taught the principal." At that point, you may have skimmed the rest of the paragraph, thinking about a funny story that involved a principal. I hope you enjoyed that moment, and hopefully now you're back.

If you need appointments at a chiropractor or masseur, you may be *listening to affirm*. Consider this HR director:

> *Grace is a nodder. She is such a caring person that she adopts new hires at the central office and takes them to lunch. It's just who she is. I do wonder sometimes if she is really processing what I say when I talk to her. She nods a lot—sometimes even uttering little "uh-huhs" and "mm-mmms" as I speak. I definitely feel heard after I talk to Grace, but I don't get a lot of substance. She's the gal I go to if I'm not sure I made the right decision. I always leave knowing I did.*

This listener is so busy responding with physical "yeses" (vertical head nods) and "nos," (horizontal head nods) she has little cognitive energy to help the other person think.

The final listening setaside articulated by cognitive coaches is *listening to inquire.* Inquisitive people can be quite engaging, but it is tough sometimes to articulate when the questions morphed from being about the coachee to being about the coach.

> *Jay is a gregarious learner. The teachers he supervises sometimes refer to him as a young puppy. Sometimes he gets so excited about an idea he gets lost in his rapid-fire questions: "That is such a great idea! Have you shared that in collaborative team? Did you put it in the V-drive? The X-drive? The Google folder? Have you tweeted it yet? I'd really love to get a copy of that for my files. You know what we could do now? We could . . ." Jay loves to learn so much his own questions get in the way of listening to others.*

Colleagues sometimes have their learning co-opted by infectious learners. These inquisitive folks really mean well and often don't know they have a listening setaside to practice.

Why these listening setasides are germane to improving written feedback is about point of view. We can replace each "listening" with "observing":

- Observing to solve problems
- Observing to tell stories
- Observing to affirm
- Observing to ask questions

In my estimation, none of these are appropriate for written feedback that will not include a face-to-face conference. Instead, just like a cognitive coach *listens to understand,* we can *observe to understand.* Then we will resist pointing a finger with "you" or co-opting the spotlight with "I" or "me."

A byproduct of really good listening is a complete focus away from yourself. This learned behavior, and framing what you see and hear in passive voice, helps move an observer from Level 2 to Level 1 (Table 5.7).

Level 1 Feedback

Table 5.7 Point of View: Level 1 Feedback

	1	2	3	4
Point of View *Purpose:* to accept the feedback more about practice than the person	Feedback primarily focuses on **actions** instead of the teacher. Passive voice pervades the feedback. *"The ACTIVBoard was used to model the Circle Map."*	Feedback is primarily written focusing on the **observer.** *"I observed that the ACTIVBoard was used to model the Circle Map."*	Feedback is primarily written from **another person's** point of view. *"You used the ACTIVBoard to model the Circle Map."* *"The teacher used the ACTIVBoard to model the Circle Map."* *"Ms. Smith used the ACTIVBoard to model the Circle Map."*	

Active vs. Passive Voice

By talking to people who learned English in a country other than the United States, we clearly notice their need for assistance in mainstreaming their syntax with that of natives. Entire businesses have emerged that assist businesses by training their customer service representatives to speak English in ways that their clients in the United States will understand. These employees are trained to use a more active voice with their customers.

Active voice emphasizes the *person* doing the action.

"Call me at 712–555–1212 if you have questions."

Active voice is direct, strong, and pointed. Americans using active voice can be interpreted as brash or even confrontational.

Passive voice emphasizes the *receiver* of the action.

"If you have questions, 712–555–1212 is where I can be reached."

Passive voice is indirect and can appear weak. However, in India, passive voice communicates deference and respect.

Consider Table 5.8 with classroom situations framed as active vs. passive.

Some English teachers or recovering grammarians throw up in their throat a bit when they read "passive voice." It is commonplace strategy for teachers of writing to avoid passive voice like the plague. However, when the doer of the action is clear, passive voice is an acceptable option (Toadvine et al., 2015). Considering the audience of teacher evaluation narratives, the teacher, it is logical to assume that the teacher will recognize the subject in most sentences that describe his classroom.

For many feedback writers, the shift to passive voice will not feel Herculean. Table 5.9 represents an assistant principal's before and after with changes italicized.

A few notes about the example:

1. This Level 3 feedback consistently uses second person ("you"). Level 2 feedback would read similarly except each time "you" appears, it would be prefaced with an "I notice" or something similar. Both feedback versions are clumsy because they use active voice.

Table 5.8 Active vs. Passive Voice

Active Voice	Passive Voice
The teacher passed out the papers, one at time, to the class of 32 students.	Each of the 32 students received their papers one at a time.
Ms. Smith organized the students into four groups of six, giving each student a role in the cooperative learning activity.	Students were grouped into four groups of six, each student with a role in the cooperative learning activity.
You spoke 90% of the time in the parent conference.	The parent listened 90% of the time in the conference, speaking more than one sentence only once.

Table 5.9 Before and After

Before	After (more passive voice)
Students are engaged and excited about learning this material. They immediately began chattering about the graph even though *you wanted them to* quietly study it first—this shows their excitement! *You* quickly addressed off-task behavior without stopping instruction. *You* have a relaxed, nurturing demeanor with *your* students *that* fosters positive relationships and a higher level of learning—they want to do well for you!	Students are engaged and excited about learning this material. They immediately began chattering about the graph even though *they were instructed* to quietly study it first—this shows their excitement! Off-task behavior *was quickly addressed* without stopping instruction. A relaxed, nurturing demeanor with students fosters positive relationships and a higher level of learning—they want to do well for you!

2. Critics of using passive voice in academic writing list wordiness as a deterrent. In the above example, passive voice actually decreased the word count!

3. This example is deficient in other desired outcomes from the High-Quality Feedback Innovation Configuration Map: description in particular. No evidence was provided for a "relaxed, nurturing demeanor," "positive relationships," or "higher level of learning."

4. The last phrase "to do well for you" breaks the passive voice and names the teacher. However, that particular sentence cannot be constructed without using "you."

As we remind ourselves of the purpose of using passive voice *(to accept the feedback more about practice than the person)*, remember Kendria's words from earlier in the chapter: "Took myself out of it." Read the "After" from the Table 5.9 again and picture this teacher reading her feedback like she forgot her reading glasses: the text in one hand extended as far away from her eyes as possible. With the exception of the last phrase, it is very possible to successfully remove yourself.

Learning, Not Teaching

I remember the first time I considered the term "teaching and learning." In a previous school district, I was asked to lead curriculum and professional development efforts. "Director of Curriculum and Professional Development" certainly was a contender but the winning option was "Director of Teaching and Learning."

That was 2004. As the standards-based movement gained traction and momentum, "teaching and learning" became such a default phrase (similar to other terms in our profession: cooperative learning, differentiation, rigor) that writers began to call its bluff: "But let's face it: It's easier to concern yourself with teaching than with learning, just as it's more convenient to say the fault lies with people other than you when things go wrong" (Kohn, 2008).

In his *Education Week* post entitled "It's Not What We Teach; It's What They Learn," Alfie Kohn (2008) relates his thinking to educational leaders:

> Finally, as teachers are to students, so administrators are to teachers. Successful school leadership doesn't depend on what principals and superintendents do, but on how their actions are regarded by their audience—notably, classroom teachers. Those on the receiving end may be older, but the moral is the same: It's best to see what we do through the eyes of those to whom it's done.
>
> (Republished with permission of Alfie Kohn)

Looking back, I wished my title had been "Director of Learning and Teaching." I have no delusions a title would have caused change in others; rather, I believe *my* priorities and decisions would have been appropriately colored by the focus on learning.

Using passive voice to write feedback to teachers focuses on learning, more than teaching. The *receivers* of the actions, the students, benefit when we focus on them and report our descriptions to their teachers.

Downey and her colleagues (2004) popularized classroom walk-throughs with the text *The Three-Minute Classroom Walk-Through*. If the title wasn't enough to lure school leaders to engage, a tight five-step process (accomplished in three minutes) was another enticement:

Step 1: Student Orientation to the Work
Step 2: Curricular Decision Points
Step 3: Instructional Decision Points
Step 4: "Walk the Walls": Curricular and Instructional Decisions
Step 5: Safety and Health Issues

(p. 21)

The wording of Step 1 might make it appear that it could be about learning—it's not. "Step 1 should be very brief, and its only purpose is to notice if students are instructionally oriented" (Downey et al., 2004, p. 23).

Downey's framework became a lightning rod for adaptations and "tweaks." I remember the very first walkthrough form I ever used: 100% of the items were environmental (e.g., presence of word walls, orientation of student desks, posted learning standard). I could have observed this classroom *sans students* and still been successful in terms of the form.

Some walkthrough forms have yet to change—still focusing either on environment, the teacher's actions, or both. However, other templates have shifted their focus from teacher to student—from teaching to learning. This is a cue for observers as they write teacher evaluation narratives.

"I always write my walkthroughs that way, but I never thought the formatives might be that way, too." This Georgia principal had the skills and experience to practice description, focus on students, and choose passive voice when needed. She simply needed to grant herself permission to transfer those effective skills.

Putting It All Together

Table 5.10 High-Quality Feedback Innovation Configuration Map

Description	1	2	3	4
Purpose: to see and hear what's going on in a classroom	Feedback is highly **descriptive**, balancing rich descriptions of student behaviors and teacher behaviors. Feedback includes **data** that was seen and heard, using direct **quotations** when appropriate. *"Three students put their heads down during the 10-minute movie, near the 6-minute mark. You remained at the back of the room speaking once to a student. It appeared that 10 students wrote something down. One student near the door used a Flow Map."*	Feedback is mostly **descriptive**, including **approximations** for what was seen and/or heard. Feedback may include student behaviors as well as teacher behaviors. *"Three students slept during the 10-minute movie. You remained at the back of the room watching the movie with the students."*	Feedback uses primarily **evaluative** and **interpretive** language. Feedback may include student behaviors as well as teacher behaviors. *"Students appeared off-task and bored during the movie despite your directions for them to take notes."*	Feedback primarily draws on **evaluative** language. Feedback is limited to teacher behaviors. *"You allowed the sleeping students too long before you intervened."*

Conditional language *Purpose:* to ponder a possible gap in practice	Conditional language is effectively used to help the reader **deeply consider gaps** or unintended results. *"At least three standards in this observation seem to be affected by students' responsibilities when they arrive to class."*	Conditional language is effectively used that would spur the reader to **pause and consider.** *"It seems that there may be a connection between instructional time and classroom routines."*	Conditional language is used to offer **suggestions.** *"We are curious about the potential if students had a consistent routine every time they entered their room."*	**Rhetorical questions** are used to suggest. *"What might happen if you had something up on the interactive whiteboard the first moment students entered the room?"*
Point of View *Purpose:* to accept the feedback more about practice than the person	Feedback primarily focuses on **actions** instead of the teacher. Passive voice pervades the feedback. *"The ACTIVBoard was used to model the Circle Map."*	Feedback is primarily written focusing on the **observer.** *"I observed that the ACTIVBoard was used to model the Circle Map."*	Feedback is primarily written from **another person's** point of view. *"**You** used the ACTIVBoard to model the Circle Map."* *"**The teacher** used the ACTIVBoard to model the Circle Map."* *"**Ms. Smith** used the ACTIVBoard to model the Circle Map."*	

A solid foundation in description, combined with judicious use of conditional language, all framed in passive voice creates successful conditions for the reader, the teacher, to sound like this:

- *Acknowledgement. Clear evidence you, the observer, were fully present in my room, working hard just like I was.*

- *Respect. Fewer directive statements, instead focusing on creating opportunities to consider some of my possible gaps.*

- *Distance. We are always teachers: in the dimly lit aisles at the grocery store, in the workout room at the gym, even at the neighborhood pool in the summer. It is sometimes hard to gain distance from our profession. Having a brief moment to step away from my classroom is a rare joy.*

Here is a sample of Level 1 feedback in the three desired outcomes from Chapters 3–5:

Instructional Strategies

During the read-aloud that was finishing up in the first three minutes of the observation, three students were reading in their own books— different than the read-aloud. Consider how you might provide more purpose for the read-aloud so students can be actively involved.

"Did anyone have strategies for how they read together during book clubs?"

- *took turns*
- *every other paragraph*
- *went back into the book to answer questions*
- *cooperate*

"Raise your hand if you used one of these Book Club Guiding Questions."

During this observation, students responded to probes over 25 times. One time the student's answer was paraphrased using different words. One time the answer was met with a smile and a laugh. Each of the other student responses was followed with the exact words being repeated aloud. When this repeating strategy is singularly used, students will eventually not listen to each other because they will rely on the repeat.

Book Clubs are new this year in fifth grade. Students report the following:

- *"I like book clubs. This time I got to choose. Last time I didn't."*
- *"Reading in school is better than doing worksheets."*
- *"I'm glad that I get to talk to my classmates about my book."*

Reading aloud is usually done with frustration-level text. Since these books are at students' independent levels, reading aloud does not increase their comprehension. Some other options students might use in lieu of reading aloud in their book clubs:

1. *"Let's read two pages, then stop."*
2. *"Let's read until we find out . . ."* (based on perhaps a continuous prediction chart for the whole book, which can be a helpful formative and summative assessment tool)
3. *"Let's read for X minutes."*

Differentiated Instruction

When asked, two students clearly articulated they were assigned a book based on their reading level.

Assessment Strategies

"In listening to your book groups yesterday, I noticed some mixing up between similes and metaphors." A mini-lesson about figurative language was then offered.

Assessment Uses

Students had difficulty coming up with metaphors on their own, decontextualized from a more complete text. Four times students raised their hands and offered inaccurate responses as metaphor examples. When they persistently had problems, an object ("dress") was offered as both a simile and a metaphor to ease their gap. It may be more productive for students to open their book club books, scan for three minutes, searching for a metaphor.

It also seemed there may not have been clear definitions used for both simile and metaphor. This site may be a helpful hint explaining to fifth graders that similes and metaphors aren't that different; in fact all similes are metaphors: http://www.dailywritingtips.com/what-is-the-difference-between-metaphor-and-simile

Positive Learning Environment

"Very proud of you guys—good talking going on. Not talking about your weekend plans, talking about the book."

"Move to the same area you were in last time. Don't move until I say go. You will have 30 seconds to get organized." After 25 seconds, students were reminded they were meeting expectations.

Academically Challenging Environment

Goal-setting with students was evident: "In your book groups, what are three things you did well?"

Student responses:

- asked questions of each other
- read together
- asked for each other's opinions on the questions
- share the book and not argue about spots

"What could you work on today in your groups? I challenge you today to use at least three of these prompts."

Twenty minutes was spent in the classroom diligently collecting description, followed by 15 minutes of adding any interpretation and evaluation. Thirty-five minutes later, this feedback was sent to this teacher who is now successfully positioned to autosupervise.

Try It Yourself

1. Examine previous feedback you have written. What is your consistent point of view default? Are you consistent within feedback narratives? Across feedback narratives?

2. Observe a class for 10 minutes and write the feedback using three different points of view (e.g., "You," "The teacher," "Ms. Smith"). Ask the leadership team to rank order their preference. Then offer the same piece of feedback framed with passive voice, more focused on students and their actions rather than the teacher.

3. Use the "Find" feature on a word processing program when writing feedback, searching for "I," "me," and "you." Re-word these phrases in passive voice and set a goal for the next narrative.

4. Practice writing passive voice during a teacher planning session or a district principal's or assistant principal's meeting. Be bold: ask a colleague to come to a faculty meeting and collect data for you, crafting feedback with description and passive voice (no conditional language). Review the collected data with your leadership team using a text-based protocol, such as *Text Rendering* (http://schoolreforminitiative.org/doc/text_rendering.pdf), or *Three Levels of Text* (http://schoolreforminitiative.org/doc/3_levels_text.pdf). Discuss implications for future faculty meetings based on the discussion.

5. Consider your learning from this chapter: What practices from this chapter are 10-degree changes? Which might require a 90-degree change in your practice? What might be first on your docket?

Reference List

Costa, A.L., & Garmston, R.J. (2002). *Cognitive coaching: A foundation for renaissance schools.* Norwood, MA: Christopher-Gordon.

Downey, C.J., Steffy, B.E., English, F.W., Frase, L.E., & Poston, Jr., W.K. (2004). *The three-minute classroom walk-through: Changing school supervisory practice one teacher at a time.* Thousand Oaks, CA: Corwin Press.

Kohn, A. (September 10, 2008). It's not what we teach, it's what they learn. *Education Week*. Retrieved from http://www.edweek.org/ew/articles/2008/09/10/03kohn_ep.h28.html.

Toadvine, A., Brizee, A., & Angeli, E. (2015). *Active and passive voice*. Retrieved from https://owl.english.purdue.edu/owl/owlprint/539/.

6 | Explicitly Owning and Raising Assumptions

Language matters. The skills we explored in the last several chapters about description, conditional language, and point of view all create the conditions where a greater probability exists that teachers will use the feedback toward professional improvements.

Each desired outcome on the High-Quality Feedback Innovation Configuration Map benefits both the writer (the observer) and the reader (the teacher), as detailed in Table 6.1.

It is not uncommon for leaders to work on school culture with and for adults. Various surveys and some leader evaluation systems use perception data from faculties and staffs to quantify the importance of school culture. However, many leaders have not specifically and explicitly determined what about their *written feedback* either perpetuates or deters a positive school culture among the adults. It is quite possible some healthy elements of school culture (e.g., recognition of achievements, collaboration on decision-making) are overshadowed or, at the very least, affected by the leader's practices in crafting written feedback.

In these cases, often our assumptions plague us as we seek to continuously improve. Teachers assume that leaders don't want to know about the quality of their written feedback, as there are not specific questions about that practice on the school culture survey. On the reciprocal end, a leader may have never contemplated asking his staff about the quality and helpfulness of his written feedback practices. These dark places of leadership rarely see the light.

Table 6.1 Mutual Benefits

Desired Outcome	Benefits for Writer/Observer	Benefits for Reader/Teacher
Descriptive Language	• Clear focus and job while observing • License to not spend precious classroom observation time engaged in constructing suggestions	• Another pair of eyes and ears • Objective data to consider • Evidence the observer worked hard
Conditional Language	• Language to create clear delineations between required and optional changes	• Less definitive language for a willing spirit to consider changes
Point of View	• Consistent voice when writing • Push to examine actions	• Temporary distance from the classroom where they spend a majority of their waking hours

For some readers, you have already identified a 90-degree shift in your practice to craft written feedback that will help teachers know and learn more about their practice and their students. Upon reflection, you now realize your past narratives were full of unhelpful summaries and countless broad generalizations. As your writing now sports your descriptive chops, proficiency with conditional language use, and a consistent, receptive point of view, it is time to see what else might fill that 20% composed of interpretation and evaluation.

There are times when providing rich description may not be enough for the reader, the teacher, to see what you may be seeing. But, that doesn't make intuitive sense, does it? Doesn't description do exactly that—provide the teacher with the evidence of what you saw and heard during the observation?

Notice the use of a very small conditional word in the last paragraph: "may." Perhaps you've observed and wondered about one of these situations:

1. *I think these are students are grouped by readiness.*

2. *I'm not sure, but I think students of color are more hesitant to participate.*

3. *Are all the students with disabilities sitting at the same two tables?*

4. *Does this teacher always act like this during collaborative planning?*

You weren't sure how to integrate this into your observation narrative besides highlighting these with description. With ample description to hold up these interpretive or evaluative statements, they could sound more like this:

1. *According to students, every group rotates to each center. It appears they complete the same work at each location. Based on Lexile levels of books students were reading in various groups, it appears that the groups may be grouped by readiness.*

2. *Based on the frequency chart above of who chose to voluntarily ask questions during the class discussion, it is possible that students of color are more hesitant to participate.*

3. *During the work period, the co-teacher interacted with the back two tables. Based on memory of names and caseloads, it seems that all students with disabilities are seated at the back two tables.*

4. *As each teacher in the collaborative planning session participated multiple times during the protocol examining student work, six times the word "Pass" was used. It is unclear the purposes you may have had for consistently passing while each of the other members consistently participated.*

This chapter builds on the other three desired outcomes from Chapters 3–5 in order to artfully pose assumptions that may be operating in classrooms. This skill takes repeated attempts to build proficiency.

Surfacing Assumptions

One of my colleagues talks about "surfacing assumptions," indicating that these thoughts are down there somewhere, perhaps in the watery abyss. Our job is to shine a light there and beckon them to rise to the surface.

Husband: [walking in after work, looking around] "It looks like you and the kids had a great day!"

Wife: "What do you mean?"

Husband: "Well, the kids really got into their toy boxes today. Over there all over the floor—I haven't seen some of those toys for quite awhile."

Wife: "So, what are you trying to say?"

Husband: [ponders] "Ooh—I think I hear one of the boys calling. Coming!"

This husband opened with an assumption: the house's cleanliness equaled a great day for both the mother and the children. After he realized (albeit late) he had stepped too quickly into that conversation, he tried using description as evidence. Too late.

Sometimes assumptions are blurted into conversation, just like this husband, without a clear lead-in. With clear understanding about the impact of articulating assumptions, a different interaction could have occurred:

Husband: [walking in after work, looking around] "Hi, honey. Wow! There are the walkie talkies. We were looking for those on the weekend."

Wife: "Well, we clearly know where they are now, and almost everything else, too."

Husband: "They sure unearthed quite a few things. Ooh—I even see they found the Nerf gun they were missing. So, it is unclear whether all of this exploring was a good thing or a bad thing."

Wife: "Actually, they really enjoyed it. I was just too tired to make them clean it all up."

Husband: "How about I go round them up now and I'll help them?"

Particular discussion protocols have specific steps to raise assumptions. Consider the *Consultancy* protocol (Dunne et al., n.d.), where a presenter brings a dilemma of practice to a group. In this experience, the educator shares some of their thinking where they might be stuck. Dilemmas differ from problems in that dilemmas are not easily solvable. If they were, the presenter would have already solved them. After hearing from the presenter, clarifying questions are asked for the participants to make sure they understand the nuts and bolts of a situation. Probing questions are for the benefit of the presenter to help him/her explore the dilemma from various points of view. The next step involves the group "borrowing" the dilemma, speaking as if it was theirs. In this step, notice the third probe in the list of discussion questions:

- What did we hear that may be important?
- What didn't we hear?
- What assumptions does this dilemma raise?
- What questions do we now have?
- What might we do if faced with a similar dilemma?

Educators frequently mention at the conclusion of protocols such as the *Consultancy* that it feels quite risky to raise possible assumptions. "I'm not sure how to start." So, when I facilitate this experience, I offer sentence starters for participants to consider:

- An assumption I hear . . .
- An assumption I hold . . .
- An assumption that may be operating . . .

Having facilitated, participated, and presented in hundreds of dilemma-based protocols, I can attest to the power of hearing assumptions. It is probable that 100% are not correct; in fact, if they were, they might not really be assumptions! Assumptions fall into the "I" of our DIE acronym: interpretation. Interpretation by its very definition means there will be differences of opinion and sometimes we will get it wrong. Therein lies the heart of the risk.

After reading and studying Chapters 3–4, you might now be quite adept at using description and then applying some conditional language to suggestions. However, there is an assumption in that very move: the reader, the teacher, will see the descriptive evidence as enough to give the suggestion a try.

As leaders seek to develop more educators that can fall into the auto-supervision bucket, we must face the reality that giving suggestions (even with wonderful conditional language attached) to reflective practitioners does not increase their reflective capacities. In some ways, it stunts it.

Consider the written feedback in Table 6.2 and how it was reframed:

The original meets many desired outcomes: description, conditional language, consistent point of view. It might even feel good writing it, particularly the last paragraph. Offering three solid ideas seems like a gift to a teacher, right?

Table 6.2 Reframed Feedback

Original	Reframed with an articulated assumption
Of the 21 students, 13 immediately made a choice from the choice board and began working. Eight students experienced various degrees of delay after students were directed to "Go for it." It took 11 minutes for all 21 students to work independently. As choice boards are more frequently implemented into instructional plans, consider how support can be provided to students who have trouble making decisions and choices. Perhaps certain students have a partner they need to report their choice to within 30 seconds of the assignment, perhaps a class tally is posted where each student publicly records their choice, perhaps a quick go round of the class before they leave the carpet asking each student: "What will you do first?"	Of the 21 students 13 immediately made a choice from the choice board and began working. Eight students experienced various degrees of delay after students were directed to "Go for it." It took 11 minutes for all 21 students to work independently. As choice boards are more frequently implemented into instructional plans, consider how support can be provided to students who have trouble making decisions and choices. _The choice boards are quite new (according to the students). It is an assumption that eight-year-olds can make instantaneous choices without learning how to first._

What the original does not do is pursue the possible root of the situation: students not being gradually exposed and scaffolded to the expectation of making choices. The underlined section of the reframed feedback replaces the idea-generation with a thoughtful assumption.

I have found that most teachers who are ready to autosupervise do not need three more ideas (even really good ones). They probably had at least 17 to start and chose one for that lesson. Adding three more is not really a value-add. What will jumpstart their thinking more is the surfacing of a possible assumption—even one that may be wrong.

What If I'm Wrong?

The evaluation system in the state of Georgia prior to 2015 usually included one 30-minute observation for an experienced teacher and three 30-minute observations for newer teachers or a teacher in need of additional support. Considering the one "dog and pony show" observation, let's do the math:

180 school days
6 teaching hours (7 hours in school minus lunch, planning, transition times)
60 minutes in an hour
2 30-minute segments in each hour
2 + 6 + 180 = 2,160 possible 30-minute observable segments
1 / 2,160 = .05% of teaching time is observed

Teacher evaluation reforms have increased the number of observations. Using Georgia as a test case, the state-mandated teacher evaluation system in 2015 requires two 30-minute segments plus four 15-minute segments = 2 hours in all. Although these segments are not observed sequentially, the math is the same:

180 school days
6 teaching hours (7 hours in school minus lunch, planning, transition times)
3 possible 2-hour segments
3 × 180 = 540 possible two-hour segments
1 / 540 = 1.9% of teaching time is observed

Of course, we're going to be wrong some of the time. We would not test-drive a car for 15–30 seconds and then pay full sticker price. Similarly, only seeing .05%–1.9% of a teacher's work does not give us a complete picture of a teacher's work with her students. This is why description forms 80% of the product, with interpretation (including assumptions) and evaluation forming the remainder. A culture of frequent feedback that has these proportions buttresses teachers as they move toward autosupervision.

Innovation Configuration Map

The desired outcome of **Assumptions** has only three iterations: the ideal (Level 1) and two other possibilities (Table 6.3). Notice that in all three possibilities, assumptions are present. It is not realistic to claim that this desired outcome does not apply to you because you don't make any assumptions.

Table 6.3 Desired Outcome: Assumptions

	1	2	3	4
Assumptions *Purpose:* to acknowledge the observer has a partial picture	Assumptions inherent in the feedback are **explicitly** identified. *"Students identified that group composition sometimes changes. The grouping rationale today was difficult to ascertain."*	Assumptions are drawn from observational evidence. The assumptions are **not recognized** nor identified by the observer. *"Flexible groups are used to offer students more opportunities to learn with others."*	Assumptions are drawn from the **lack of observational evidence.** The assumptions are not recognized nor identified by the observer. *"Consider having the groups organized in more intentional ways based on assessment."*	

Level 3 Feedback

A recent interaction with an assistant principal exemplifies this desired outcome (Table 6.4). After learning with him over the course of a summer professional development session, he had become aware of his ever-burgeoning assumptions. This learning disarmed him, and he was really worried that his relationships with teachers would suffer because of it. So, he set a goal for himself: not have any. My response a few months into the year: "How's that goin' for ya?"

We re-tooled his goal into the following: "I will become more aware of my assumptions and learn how to articulate them." His specific action steps included asking this question before any teacher or parent conference he had over the next three weeks: "What do I assume to be true right now?"

Table 6.4 Assumptions: Level 3 Feedback

	1	2	3	4
Assumptions *Purpose:* to acknowledge the observer has a partial picture			Assumptions are drawn from the **lack of observational evidence.** The assumptions are not recognized nor identified by the observer. *"Consider having the groups organized in more intentional ways based on assessment."*	

"No one person or perspective can give us the answers we need to the problems of today. Paradoxically, we can only find those answers by admitting we don't know. We have to be willing to let go of our certainty and expect ourselves to be confused for a time" (Wheatley, 2002, p. 34) The purpose of making assumptions clear in written feedback is to acknowledge the observer has a partial picture. Although many assumptions fall into interpretation, they can easily teeter into evaluation:

It is unclear why you gave the students instructions as they were walking back to their desks.

Margaret Wheatley so eloquently nudges us: "It's not differences that divide us. It's our judgments about each other that do. Curiosity and good listening bring us back together" (2002, p. 36).

Table 6.5 Level 3 Feedback and Something Better

Level 3 Feedback	Better Iteration
Yesterday's assessment was used formatively to create a tiered lesson in today's Senior Economics class. A high, medium, and low group each worked toward the same KUD (know/understand/do), with differing levels of support. *Each group did not work with the same engagement. Perhaps the quality of the tasks were not equally respectful.*	Yesterday's assessment was used formatively to create a tiered lesson in today's Senior Economics class: "Based on yesterday's quiz, today we will . . ." A high, medium, and low group each worked toward the same KUD (know/understand/do), with differing levels of support.
	Each group did not work with the same engagement. The group with the most open-ended assignment only discussed economics-related topics. Students in the lowest tiers did not work together; they worked parallel to each other in separate desks. One student received individual instruction for eight minutes. Two students, T and G, never joined their group (lowest). Instead they discussed the weather and college admissions for the entire work period. When asked why they were probably assigned to that group: "We missed the quiz and aren't allowed to make any up."
	The grouping strategies for most students were based on assessment results. However, for T and G, a lack of one specific assessment result placed them in a group that may not have fit their academic needs.

Generally Speaking

Part of the job as a leader is to move from specific to general:

- I have two parent complaints about students getting onto bus 42 on time; therefore, the whole bus dismissal procedure may be problematic.
- There are more student referrals from a teacher's fifth period class than any of her other periods. She's having classroom management problems in fifth period.

A generalizing statement is not automatically untrue, just like an assumption is not automatically untrue. In fact, generalizing seems to be a job necessity in some contexts and a job hazard in others.

Classroom teachers do not generally look favorably on leaders who frequently generalize. The risk is too high and the probability of inaccurately lumping is too great. Reminders at a staff meeting about making sure teachers sign in every morning fall flat when the teacher grapevine has it on good authority (from someone in the front office) that only two teachers are inconsistent. Impassioned pleas to the whole staff from the special education department about accurately implementing accommodations often ricochet off the few teachers not complying, instead causing those that *are* implementing with fidelity to question their decisions.

The italicized assumption in the Level 3 feedback found in Table 6.5 does not have observational evidence. The first sentence poses an interpretation ("same engagement") unsupported by description and is followed by an assumption.

This piece of feedback stems from a school that studied differentiation and knew some things: tiered lesson, KUD, equally respectful tasks. Sometimes teachers like to pose the credibility issue to observers: "When was the last time you were in a classroom?" Although this economics teacher could pose that same question here, there is not a clear gap between the pedagogical knowledge of the observer and the teacher (at least in this short snippet).

That being said, using terms correctly does not equate to highly effective feedback. Notice how the better iteration included more description of the engagement, asked students to garner more data, and then posed an assumption that still acknowledged a partial picture while creating some cognitive dissonance for the teacher.

Level 2 Feedback

In working with educators, I have generally found them quite adept at identifying description. For instance, when I hold up a half-full plastic water bottle, these are the usual responses when they are asked to describe it:

- I see a lid.
- I see a blue label.
- I see a half-full bottle.
- [of course] I see a half-empty bottle.

As soon as someone ventures into the liquid inside the bottle, groups often throw a red flag: *I see water.* What evidence do you have? Just because there is clear liquid inside a water bottle does not necessarily make it water. In fact, I see a clear difference when working with high school leaders: they are much quicker to doubt the liquid is water. Ask any experienced high school assistant principal what clear liquids they have found in a water bottle and the answer is not limited to water.

Table 6.6 Assumptions: Level 2 Feedback

	1	2	3	4
Assumptions *Purpose:* to acknowledge the observer has a partial picture		Assumptions are drawn from observational evidence. The assumptions are **not recognized** nor identified by the observer. *"Flexible groups are used to offer students more opportunities to learn with others."*	Assumptions are drawn from the **lack of observational evidence.** The assumptions are not recognized nor identified by the observer. *"Consider having the groups organized in more intentional ways based on assessment."*	

However, the isolated practice on a water bottle does not always successfully transfer when observers attempt written feedback (Table 6.6). Stone and Heen (2014) articulate three leaks in our façade that make it difficult for us to spot:

- leaky face
- leaky tone
- leaky patterns

The leaky tone is the most apropos here. The authors reference face-to-face feedback in their explanations of leaky tone, but the metaphor translates to written feedback quite well. Stone and Heen consider how infants use the superior temporal sulcus (STS) to process what they hear: "At four months all auditory information—whether their mother's voice or a car horn—is attended to by the STS. . . . This little piece of our brain is dedicated to taking in language and reading tone and meaning . . . When we ourselves speak, the STS *turns off*" (p. 83, italics original).

Turns off?! This explains how often we might receive feedback on our tone—not the words we speak but the *how* they are delivered. We simply don't hear the tone.

Writing is full of tone. Ask educators who have received an email that made them want them to spit, vomit, cry, or hit. Knowing that our writing is tone-filled is critical to how we approach our assumption-checking. *Just because we think it's description, doesn't make it so.*

The learning hits home for me as a vocalist. Five years of college voice lessons certainly impressed in me the lie I had been living: *I know what I sound like.* Mrs. De Haan would always ask: "How did that *feel* to you?," never "How did that *sound* to you?" She knew where I needed to place my tongue on vowels, how I should raise my palate, when I needed to sing more through "the mask." Unfortunately, she could not surgically cross-section my head to see all the placements. Instead she needed to rely on her vast vocal pedagogy experience triangulated with how I thought it felt. Now it's time to apply that learning to our written feedback.

Look at Table 6.7 and see if you can identify the implicit assumption.

Table 6.7 Level 2 Feedback and Something Better

Level 2 Feedback	Better Iteration
Students were silently copying down a conversion look-up diagram, reminded to ensure that arrows were going the correct way.	Students were silently copying down a conversion look-up diagram, reminded to ensure that arrows were going the correct way.
Students will experience difficulty using the chart for several reasons:	*Although this observation did not include independent practice of conversions, it is probable* students *may* experience difficulty using the chart for several reasons:
On initial viewing, the chart seems quite helpful. It is also a bit counter-intuitive—multiply when you start with a bigger unit, divide when you start with a smaller unit.	On initial viewing, the chart seems quite helpful. It is also a bit counter-intuitive—multiply when you start with a bigger unit, divide when you start with a smaller unit.
Later when students tried to use the diagram to convert, the trickiness grew:	Later when students tried to use the diagram to convert, the trickiness grew:
The first example:____ centimeter = 5 meters is tricky as a first example: students need to read right to left in order to see what they have because the unknown value is on the left side.	The first example:____ centimeter = 5 meters is tricky as a first example: students need to read right to left in order to see what they have because the unknown value is on the left side.
Another reason that problem is tricky is because, in the problem, centimeter is to the left of meter, but in the diagram centimeter is to the right of meter.	Another reason that problem is tricky is because, in the problem, centimeter is to the left of meter, but in the diagram centimeter is to the right of meter.

Students will experience difficulty using the chart for several reasons.

Notice in the better iteration, more description was not needed to ameliorate this problem. Instead, the italicized portion addressed the gap that placed this feedback in Level 2: not being explicit about the assumptions—making sure you are aware they are truly there. In other words, knowing what you sound like by the feel, not relying on the sound. This was accomplished in the better iteration by acknowledging the partial picture.

Imagine all the outcomes that could occur if this teacher received this feedback in a timely way:

- If independent practice occurred after the observer left, the feedback may explain the frustration the students exhibited.
- If the students were able to successfully maneuver through the assignment, the assumption is disregarded, but offering the problem from the student's perspective may still live on in the teacher's mind.
- If she scheduled independent practice for tomorrow, another whole group mini-lesson may allay misconceptions.

After improving at each of the desired outcomes articulated in Chapters 3–6 through hundreds of classroom observations, I can feel an assumption in my hand as I type it. I don't hear it in my head when I'm inaudibly narrating what I'm going to write next. The assumptions actually make it past that filter and almost onto the page.

If they do make it onto the page, I have two responsibilities:

1. own it to make it explicit, and
2. ensure I have ample description to hold it up (like walls on a house holding up the roof).

Attending to DIE helps develop an awareness of our "automatic" or "natural" responses, which "may involve assumptions that have little or no relation to the actual work students have done" (Blythe et al., 2008, p. 30).

Level 1 Feedback

Level 1 feedback in this desired outcome consistently and thoughtfully explains assumptions. An excerpt of the following example was used in Chapter 4 demonstrating descriptive language—here the entire text exemplifies this careful attention to the belief the observer only has a partial picture:

As questions were asked during the lesson, sometimes students were called on individually; other times unison response was used. When unison response was used and a question was asked immediately after the student responses, students would respond with the other answer:

T: "Is this a plant or an animal?"
many S: "Plant"

Table 6.8 Assumptions: Level 1 Feedback

	1	2	3	4
Assumptions *Purpose:* to acknowledge the observer has a partial picture	Assumptions inherent in the feedback are **explicitly** identified. *"Students identified that group composition sometimes changes. The grouping rationale today was difficult to ascertain."*	Assumptions are drawn from observational evidence. The assumptions are **not recognized** nor identified by the observer. *"Flexible groups are used to offer students more opportunities to learn with others."*	Assumptions are drawn from the **lack of observational evidence.** The assumptions are not recognized nor identified by the observer. *"Consider having the groups organized in more intentional ways based on assessment."*	

T: "How do you know it was a plant?"
many S: "Animal"

One way to avoid this flip-flopping is to preface the second question with a direction: "I just want to hear from individual students here: How do you know?" After the first Sponge Bob introduction (met with laughter and smiles), a question was asked: "Is it a plant or an animal?" After a unison response, one student offered: "Because it breathes."

T: "That's interesting—let's learn more."
Another student asked him: "How did you see it breathe?"

That second student had an important point to make: visual cues are not germane to all three of the criteria: "make food, mouth, anchored." When the four practices of determining plants/animals were offered, a narrative of one to two sentences described the situation. Students were asked whether it was a plant or an animal, then not given the right answer until the picture was shown and re-asked, "Is it a plant or an animal?" This may prove confusing for students as they apply visual cues to a task that is intended to be inferential (from the text). It is difficult to determine without talking to students if they were purely using visual cues.

Just like the *Consultancy* dilemma-discussion protocol explained earlier in this chapter, surfacing assumptions allows an educator to consider them and "begin to have a mindful relationship" (Kegan & Lahey, 2001, p. 130) with them. In the previous example about sponges, this teacher of young children can decide how, if at all, she has misapplied the science content of plants and animals by making the criteria visual. On its face, planning visually for young learners makes perfect sense, but the unintended consequence, if interpreted by her as valid, may be an important deterrent for her in future planning. She needs to decide if she holds her assumption as a truth, or if the assumption is *holding her.*

By placing an assumption like this in writing, teachers have no requirement to respond to it. It "helps the presenter get out of her own way and examine her assumptions" (Blythe et al., 2008, p. 47). That being said, I recommend that if a narrative contains more than two identified assumptions, it may be important to schedule a debrief conversation. That kind of deep thinking may feel like overload and if the purpose of giving the feedback truly aligns to accelerating improvements in classroom practice, a guided conversation may be the best route.

Deconstructive Criticism

Some of the examples in this chapter may have represented the biggest gap when comparing your pre-reading-of-this-book feedback to now. Surfacing assumptions and crafting them into written feedback may appear quite tricky. Don't be discouraged by this practice and revert into the faulty paradigm of positive/negative.

Assuming a binary system like positive/negative can be quite halting to your prowess at writing high-quality feedback. If you lived within this system, you would constantly assess your feedback to see if it is positive for the receiver.

Educators are smart folks. When I have pushed on this binary with leaders I coach, I usually receive a response similar to the following: "Well, it's not really *positive* I'm looking for—more like *constructive*. As long as it's constructive, then I'll use it in my feedback."

So, using that line of thinking, constructive has a logical binary opposite: destructive. Hendrie Weisinger (1990), a UCLA psychologist, identified four criteria for constructive and destructive feedback (Table 6.9).

In reading these two options, constructive certainly seems like the logical and appropriate choice. School leaders who are aiming for destructive feedback will not be in those positions for long.

As with any framework and correlative characteristics, assumptions exist—not surprising! Identified by Kegan and Lahey (2001), *Assumption #1: the supervisor is right.* The specific change she wants the teacher to make is

Table 6.9 Constructive vs. Destructive

Constructive	Destructive
Specific	Vague
Supportive	Blames the person
Problem solving	Threatening
Timely	Pessimistic

correct and solves a problem present in the classroom. Numerous supports may be offered to make that change happen. You might be nodding along, agreeing as you read this paragraph, thinking, 'Yes, when I indicate a change needs to be made, I do think I am right.' As with a logic test, let's check the opposite of Assumption #1: If you are right, then the perspective of the teacher must be wrong. That may make this assumption a bit harder to swallow.

Assumption #2: It is the supervisor's duty to own most of this situation. "He is the one presumably prepared to (1) say exactly what the person is doing wrong, (2) give the sense the criticism is meant to help, (3) suggest a solution, and (4) give a timely message" (Kegan & Lahey, 2001, p. 129).

If these assumptions, or anything close to them, are operating under the constructive feedback framework, then the purpose of the feedback looks quite simple, as evidenced in Figure 6.1.

Education theorists would label this the transmission model of education, certainly at odds with most prevailing models in the 21st century.

A third option exists, according to Kegan and Lahey (2001): deconstructive feedback. This stance offers a more respectful and learning-filled path than both constructive and destructive feedback. Deconstructive feedback does not seek to tear down nor build up the person or the observation; instead, it disassembles our own judgments.

Figure 6.1 Constructive Feedback Purpose

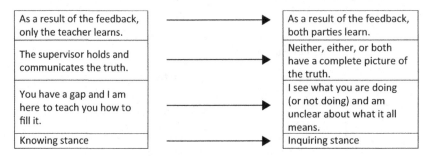

As a result of the feedback, only the teacher learns.	As a result of the feedback, both parties learn.
The supervisor holds and communicates the truth.	Neither, either, or both have a complete picture of the truth.
You have a gap and I am here to teach you how to fill it.	I see what you are doing (or not doing) and am unclear about what it all means.
Knowing stance	Inquiring stance

Figure 6.2 Shifts from Constructive to Deconstructive
Adapted from Kegan and Lahey (2001).

Deconstructive feedback validates the purpose of acknowledging a partial picture. Consider the shifts an observer would make moving from constructive to deconstructive in Figure 6.2.

Practically Speaking, or Writing

So, what does this look like in practice? How can we explicitly surface assumptions that acknowledge a partial picture and provide the richest learning conditions for the observer and the teacher?

Here are a few examples:

Twenty-four students were sitting listening to a lead-up before watching Super Bowl advertisements. This date coincided with the 30th anniversary of the Mac computer. This lead-up took 13 minutes, inclusive of a prediction that the students would not understand the Apple commercial. The actual Apple video took 30 seconds. After the video, more teacher talk occurred.

Nine questions were asked to students during this teacher-led time, eight were quantitative in nature:

How many of you have read 1984?
How many people have been out in the hall today?
How many people have been to Wal-Mart?
How many people have been inside Wal-Mart?
How many people have been on the interstate?

The results of these questions varied with some students raising their hands, but no students ever talked.

It is unclear what evidence exists to preclude student experience as a factor in understanding the 1984 commercial. By opening up those opportunities, we might discover an important misconception that could guide our instruction.

Notice the prompt, "it is unclear." That prompt and a few others below offer an entrée into writing assumptions.

- An assumption that may be operating . . .
- A possible assumption students could be making . . .

- It is unclear . . .
- Unsure if . . .
- Difficult to determine . . .

Students are very clear about words such as "mastery, learning goal, essential question, exit ticket." They were able to articulate plausible definitions when you checked for understanding. Students seemed quite nonplussed about the extra practice of elapsed time: "Kids, I looked at your homework from last night and added a center for everyone. It's about elapsed time. Because that has been tricky for us, I'm going to be at that center today." An assumption I hold is that homework is often used in formative ways, informing the lesson activities for successive days.

Sometimes assumptions do not have a deeper learning intent for the readers, the teachers. They are simply included to meet the purpose: acknowledge the observer has a partial picture. If an observer identifies an assumption on his/her own part, it may necessitate a brief foray into first person: "An assumption *I* hold is that homework . . ."

Essential Question [EQ] posted: What were the causes and consequences of exploration and colonization?
When asked what they were learning, a student replied:

- *Learning about Chris Columbus, Prince Henry the Navigator*
- *Going to different stations*
- *Learning about different explorers*

The tasks and response from the students posit an unclear connection to the EQ. It is difficult to determine if the students believe the learning is all about the explorers and less about their role in exploration and colonization. Perhaps today's learning was a prequel or a baseline experience leading to the posted EQ.

Description in this case relied heavily on student responses. After hearing how helpful it can be to hear what students are thinking, teachers who are ready to autosupervise will only have one complaint: too few students' input was included!

> *The conference began with a description of the gradebook for each of E's subjects. Each missing assignment was highlighted verbally as well as E's behavior log. The word "potential" was used at least eight times. The phrase "E chooses to" was used at least 12 times. In the 20-minute conference with E's parent, the parent spoke <5% of the time. She asked two questions, both of which were answered in one sentence each. An assumption that E's parent might have is that her experience with E at home is not relevant to our work with him at school.*

The other desired outcomes (description, conditional language, and point of view) do not offer the observer an opportunity to offer another perspective. Assumptions posed from another standpoint can be highly informative to a teacher.

Observing as Inquirers

Margaret Wheatley (2002), a leadership author, has much to teach us about how to co-inquire with classroom teachers. Consider these short quotations:

- "Curiosity is what we need. We don't have to let go of what we believe, but we need to be curious about what someone else believes" (p. 35).
- "My shock at your position exposes my own position" (p. 36).
- "When we listen with less judgment, we always develop better relationships with each other" (p. 36).

Re-worded, the last statement may be most apropos: when we *observe* with less judgment, we always develop better relationships. These relationships are, in part, formed by diligent gathering of description, careful application of conditional language, consistent use of point of view, and an explicit owning and raising of assumptions. These four skills create the conditions for teachers to truly learn and benefit from written feedback.

Putting It All Together

Table 6.10 High-Quality Feedback Innovation Configuration Map

Description	1	2	3	4
Purpose: to see and hear what's going on in a classroom	Feedback is highly **descriptive,** balancing rich descriptions of student behaviors and teacher behaviors. Feedback includes **data** that was seen and heard, using direct **quotations** when appropriate. "*Three students put their heads down during the 10-minute movie, near the 6-minute mark. You remained at the back of the room speaking once to a student. It appeared that 10 students wrote something down. One student near the door used a Flow Map.*"	Feedback is mostly **descriptive,** including **approximations** for what was seen and/or heard. Feedback may include student behaviors as well as teacher behaviors. "*Three students slept during the 10-minute movie. You remained at the back of the room watching the movie with the students.*"	Feedback uses primarily **evaluative** and **interpretive** language. Feedback may include student behaviors as well as teacher behaviors. "*Students appeared off-task and bored during the movie despite your directions for them to take notes.*"	Feedback primarily draws on **evaluative** language. Feedback is limited to teacher behaviors. "*You allowed the sleeping students too long before you intervened.*"

Conditional Language *Purpose*: to ponder a possible gap in practice	Conditional language is effectively used to help the reader **deeply consider gaps** or unintended results. *"At least three standards in this observation seem to be affected by students' responsibilities when they arrive to class."*	Conditional language is effectively used that would spur the reader to **pause and consider.** *"It seems that there may be a connection between instructional time and classroom routines."*	Conditional language is used to offer **suggestions.** *"We are curious about the potential if students had a consistent routine every time they entered their room."*	**Rhetorical questions** are used to suggest. *"What might happen if you had something up on the interactive whiteboard the first moment students entered the room?"*
Point of View *Purpose*: to accept the feedback more about practice than the person	Feedback primarily focuses on **actions** instead of the teacher. Passive voice pervades the feedback. *"The ACTIVBoard was used to model the Circle Map."*	Feedback is primarily written focusing on the **observer.** *"I observed that the ACTIVBoard was used to model the Circle Map."*	Feedback is primarily written from **another person's** point of view. *"You used the ACTIVBoard to model the Circle Map."* *"The teacher used the ACTIVBoard to model the Circle Map."* *"Ms. Smith used the ACTIVBoard to model the Circle Map."*	

(Continued)

Table 6.10 (Continued)

| **Assumptions** *Purpose:* to acknowledge the observer has a partial picture | Assumptions inherent in the feedback are **explicitly** identified.

 "Students identified that group composition sometimes changes. The grouping rationale today was difficult to ascertain." | Assumptions are drawn from observational evidence. The assumptions are **not recognized** nor identified by the observer.

 "Flexible groups are used to offer students more opportunities to learn with others." | Assumptions are drawn from the **lack of observational evidence.** The assumptions are not recognized nor identified by the observer.

 "Consider having the groups organized in more intentional ways based on assessment." | |

Rich description and thoughtful uses of conditional language, set in passive voice, with assumptions explicitly identified create successful conditions for the reader, the teacher, to sound like this:

- *Acknowledgement. What was collected (seen and heard) is helpful to read, as I miss moments when I am in the "teaching zone."*
- *Respect. My principal believes I am capable enough to think about things and doesn't need to always tell me what to do.*
- *Distance. Reading about a classroom dispassionately allows me to temper my own emotions about what is so close to me.*
- *Community. By explicitly acknowledging you don't know everything during the few and brief times you are in my room, I am more apt to accept what you have written.*

Here is a sample of Level 1 feedback in the four desired outcomes detailed in Chapters 3–6.

Instructional Strategies

Essential Question posted: What are dynamics? Dynamics were referenced three times during the observation.

Different groupings existed during the rehearsal: whole group, small groups, individual students.

When first trumpets had difficulty, the melody was sung near them to support them.

Flutes played their parts accurately but were not playing with consistent breath. They were told "to connect the sounds," immediately had an opportunity to improve, and they did.

When first trumpets continued to have difficulty, they were given opportunities to play the passages again at a slower tempo. They were told to practice at home, and after school times were made available.

Each time when students are to begin playing, a full measure is snapped and called out. This has two unintended consequences: students now have a "ramp up" time to pay attention and they learn that they do not need to look at the conductor, just listen. One preparatory beat should be enough for them to ascertain tempo and to breathe.

"Vivace is a new tempo for us. It means very fast." Consider how you might build more connections to their background knowledge when introducing Italian. So much of Italian is connected to Latin and they have multiple reasons to learn Latin roots (e.g., science, language arts). For instance, they might be asked what they see/hear in the word *Vivace* and what words it reminds them of (e.g., *vivacious, vitality = full of life*). *Vivace* really means brisk and lively and how that is played is then very fast.

Students were offered the opportunity to *"finger along"* as the song, *"Alpha Squadron,"* progressed. No students chose this option.

The new song was described as *"two melodies fighting: one lyrical and one punchy."* Two students commented on this description.

It is unclear what the process is when students don't have their instruments:

- *One student using his umbrella, making gun sounds, poking the students in front of him*
- *One student laying down in the back*
- *One student making a rainbow loom bracelet*

Assessment Strategies

Formative assessment consistently occurs throughout the observation. Students have multiple opportunities to play the same excerpt.

Assessment Uses

What may be unclear to students is why this is occurring. Assumptions might include wrong note, wrong fingering, wrong articulation. . . . Consider how you could briefly make the purpose clear. That might sound like: "Trumpets again—let's check fingerings." or "Trumpets: do it again. The fingerings are right but we need to firm up our emboucheres to hit the higher notes."

Fifteen minutes was spent in the classroom diligently collecting description, followed by 15 minutes of adding any interpretation and evaluation. Thirty minutes later, this teacher is positioned to autosupervise.

Try It Yourself

1. Access a recent written observation of a very competent teacher, searching for overtly constructive language. Work independently or with others to rewrite that in a more deconstructive way, surfacing more assumptions and assuming an inquiry stance.

2. Try the same process with a written observation that contained several strategies. Determine what assumptions might be identified to produce a similar result: a teacher considering a change of strategy.

3. Consider how to become more comfortable with the surfacing of assumptions. Try using the *Questions and Assumptions* protocol (http://schoolreforminitiative.org/doc/questions_assumptions.pdf) with a professional text that your leadership team or administrative team is reading.

4. The next time you are asking for input on a document you have created (e.g., a testing schedule, a school year calendar, new bus dismissal procedures), consider using the *Questions and Assumptions* protocol (http://schoolreforminitiative.org/doc/questions_assumptions.pdf) so staff members may grow in their comfort about raising assumptions to each other and to you.

5. If using protocols in your leadership practice looks attractive, consider an organizational structure for your learning called *Protocol Families* (http://schoolreforminitiative.org/doc/protocol_families.pdf): read about some of the "Exploring and Managing Dilemmas" protocols.

6. Read the entire chapter called "Willing to Be Disturbed" from *Turning to One Another: Simple Conversations to Restore Hope to the Future* by Margaret Wheatley. Pose a framing question as you discuss with other observers: What could we learn through classroom observations by adopting a stance more aligned with Wheatley?

7. The next time a school plan or process is developed, consider using the following structure in your written explanation or communication:

   Purpose

   Guiding Assumptions

   Rationale

Process

Steps

8. Consider your learning from this chapter: What practices from this chapter are 10-degree changes? Which might require a 90-degree change in your practice? What might be first on your docket?

Reference List

Blythe, T., Allen, D., & Powell, B.S. (2008). *Looking together at student work* (2nd ed.). New York, NY: Teachers College Press.

Dunne, F., Evans, P., & Thompson-Grove, G. (n.d.). *Consultancy.* Retrieved from http://schoolreforminitiative.org/doc/consultancy.pdf.

Kegan, R., & Lahey, L.L. (2001). *How the way we talk can change the way we work: Seven languages for transformation.* San Francisco, CA: Jossey-Bass.

Stone, D., & Heen, S. (2014). *Thanks for the feedback: The art and science of receiving feedback well.* New York, NY: Random House.

Weisinger, H. (1990). *The Critical edge: How to criticize up and down your organization and make it pay off.* New York, NY: HarperCollins.

Wheatley, M.J. (2002). *Turning to one another: Simple conversations to restore hope to the future.* San Francisco, CA: Berrett-Koshler Publishers, Inc.

7

The Trickiness of Co-Teaching Situations

Language matters. After 18 months of building shared understanding about instruction and assessment, the language that school and district leaders had developed and practiced in Decatur, Georgia, was no longer enough. During this time, leaders shared their feedback in public ways, risking the dark spaces of their leadership in order to improve. The team developed criteria to define high-quality written feedback and created a set of expectations in the form of an Innovation Configuration Map. Videos and live classroom observations of specialized content (e.g., art, music, physical education, foreign language, career technical education) were used to test our skills in contents that were unfamiliar to most. But that wasn't enough. Co-teaching was next.

Decatur was proud of its co-teaching use; in fact, it had received multiple awards from the Georgia Department of Education regarding the percentage of students who spent a majority of their school day in their least restrictive environment. This, however, did not mean that the district had shared language around co-teaching. The successful contexts were more indicative of teachers' willingness to muck around and do their best on behalf of students.

For most Decatur leaders, observations of special educators were tricky. There were four iterations that characterized how special educators were evaluated:

1. Leaders would examine a special educator's schedule and only consider observation times when students were in resource or "pull-out"

settings. Special educators often received a perceived advantage compared to regular educators: they often knew when the observations would take place.

2. Leaders would occasionally use co-teaching situations but only for the short, formative observations, relying on resource settings for the observations they seemed to "count more." These observers reported needing these resource settings because they "just couldn't gather what they needed during co-teaching."

3. Observers admitted a strategy that is probably all too frequent: "When I'm in a co-teaching setting, I only focus on one person. If they aren't teaching while I'm in there, I usually leave."

4. A quote from written feedback following a professional development session offered an assumption critical for us to hear: "I can't evaluate when two people are team teaching. That won't work."

It was clear that we didn't have shared understanding or language about co-teaching—as leaders, as teachers, as a school district. We also had a feeling this learning for leadership was going to be different. The High-Quality Feedback Innovation Configuration Map ended up changing, too.

Innovation Configuration Map

Co-teaching encompasses two desired outcomes on the Innovation Configuration Map (Table 7.1): one for **Co-Teaching Model** and one for **Co-Teaching Equity.** The desired outcome of the co-teaching model includes four iterations: the ideal (Level 1) and three other possibilities. The desired outcome of co-teaching equity uses a binary system: either the ideal or an unacceptable variation.

Level 4 Feedback

Level 4 feedback (Table 7.2) for co-teaching models may meet some of the other desired outcomes (e.g., description, conditional language, explicit

Table 7.1 Co-Teaching Model and Equity Innovation Configuration Maps

	1	2	3	4
Co-Teaching Model *Purpose:* to identify purposes and jobs of multiple adults in classrooms	In co-teaching situations, the identified co-teaching model(s) serves as a **foundation** for the feedback. *"The Tree Map drawn on the board by Ms. Smith as complementary co-teaching while you were discussing was referenced three times by students later in the discussion."*	In co-teaching situations, feedback is **related** to the co-teaching model(s) used but the model is not identified. *"Ms. Smith drew a Tree Map on the whiteboard as you discussed with students."*	In co-teaching situations, the co-teaching model(s) is identified but **disconnected** from any feedback. *"Today's lesson used the Complementary Co-Teaching model."*	In co-teaching situations, **nothing** in the feedback **reflects on the reality** of multiple adults present in the classroom. *[Feedback does not reference multiple adults in the classroom.]*
Co-Teaching Equity *Purpose:* to not reinforce hierarchies between adults	In co-teaching situations, language focuses on **equity:** on the **action** rather than the person. *"One Teach, One Observe was used. This content seems to need a co-teaching model where both adults are more actively engaged with students."*	In co-teaching situations, language suggests **power:** "having" another colleague do something. *"Consider having your co-teacher alternatively teach during your mini-lesson."*		

Table 7.2 Co-Teaching Model: Level 4 Feedback

	1	2	3	4
Co-Teaching Model *Purpose:* to identify purposes and jobs of multiple adults in classrooms				In co-teaching situations, **nothing** in the feedback **reflects on the reality** of multiple adults present in the classroom. *[Feedback does not reference multiple adults in the classroom.]*

Table 7.3 Level 4 Feedback and Something Better

Level 4 Feedback	Better Iteration
Students are being served in their areas of need. During the math lesson, some students were on the floor, some in desks, some at the interactive whiteboard. The lesson included scaffolded examples that required students to work one step at a time. Each student had multiple materials: graph paper and individual whiteboards/markers. No evidence was noted that indicates specific modifications were made for specific students.	During the math lesson, some students were on the floor, some in desks, some at the interactive whiteboard. The lesson included scaffolded examples that required students to work one step at a time. Each student had multiple materials: graph paper and individual whiteboards/markers. No evidence was noted that indicates specific modifications were made for specific students. *It is unclear which co-teaching model was used. It appeared that one was teaching and every other adult was providing individual support. Based on the frequent wrong answers during the lesson, a more active co-teaching model may have been a more strategic choice.*

assumptions), but does not acknowledge the reality of multiple adults present in a classroom. The lack of that admission automatically places this feedback in Level 4. This sort of feedback characterized the practice in Decatur for a wide preponderance of observations. Since we were unaware how to write high-quality feedback in co-teaching situations, our only recourse was to completely avoid referencing the other adults in the room.

Although we were avoiding the mention of multiple adults (Table 7.3), this behavior did not work well with the teachers receiving the feedback. Teachers were no longer sequestering their teacher evaluation ratings. Although the leaders might not reference the other adult(s) in the room, the adults aren't ignoring each other at all. It was becoming quite common for teachers, especially co-teaching pairs, to openly discuss their ratings and comments. The frequency of observations in current teacher evaluation systems has normalized this phenomenon.

Instrumental Knowing

I distinctively remember one of the very first videos we used in a professional development session. Instructional coaches at each school had been issued a small video camera and asked to collect co-teaching footage. As the agenda planners pored through hours of co-teaching video footage, we found a case of four adults being in one fourth grade classroom at the same time. We thought, 'What a ripe video for our learning!'

There was no doubt about the ripeness of the clip. Not only couldn't the group fathom how to write feedback with the multiple adults in the room, but another very intense conversation commandeered the learning. The group donned their school operations hats and wondered aloud about personnel funding and push-in support. Principals started to "do the math" (school funding math, not the math of the video) and were concerned about human capital equity between schools. Exploring co-teaching was going to be tough for us, and we might need a different kind of learning to take our next steps.

Breidenstein and her colleagues (2012) have effectively contextualized Kegan's constructive-developmental theory in schools. Kegan articulates three ways of knowing, detailed in Table 7.4.

In examining the learning artifacts of Decatur leaders, the agendas leaned toward more opportunities for participants to engage in socializing

Table 7.4 Kegan's Constructive-Developmental Theory

Instrumental Knowers	Socializing Knowers	Self-Authoring Knowers
• Have concrete needs • Believe that rules are important and search for the "right way" • Have limited interest in reflection or collaboration when their own needs are not met	• Focus on others • Believe that group needs are important • Are uncomfortable with conflicting opinions, values, and behaviors	• Are reflective about themselves and their context • Can live with ambiguity • Are able to stand in opposition to a group

knowing. Authentic video clips for study, protocols structuring the conversation for equity and effectiveness, and public sharing of written feedback all were appropriate matches for socializing knowers.

As the agenda planners consistently engaged with participants' written reflections after each session, they believed the group needed a break from socializing knowing—that didn't mean the agendas didn't include any talking with each other! Rather, we decided to not socially construct co-teaching models from our experiences, like we had developed the High-Quality Feedback Innovation Configuration Map. It seemed the group needed some instrumental knowing.

Level 3 Feedback

For instrumental knowers, their very first step involved identifying the co-teaching model(s) observed in classrooms. This may have brought their feedback to Level 3 (Table 7.5).

Identifying co-teaching models represented instrumental learning for most Decatur leaders. Although some leaders may have experienced undergraduate or graduate courses about special education at some point

Table 7.5 Co-Teaching Model: Level 3 Feedback

	1	2	3	4
Co-Teaching Model *Purpose:* to identify purposes and jobs of multiple adults in classrooms			In co-teaching situations, the co-teaching model(s) is identified but **disconnected** from any feedback. *"Today's lesson used the Complementary Co-Teaching model."*	In co-teaching situations, **nothing** in the feedback **reflects on the reality** of multiple adults present in the classroom. *[Feedback does not reference multiple adults in the classroom.]*

in their preparation programs, most of them did not retain the information due to infrequency of use.

Decatur chose to use models popularized by Marilyn Friend (Friend & Cook, 2012) in her oft-viewed video series, *The Power of 2,* and successive publications. Decatur leaders never viewed the video series, choosing to use video footage from their own schools and classrooms, but adapted her models and corresponding language as their own.

Co-Teaching Models

One Teach/One Observe: One adult delivers instruction while the other adult conducts systematic observation of students to gather meaningful data.

One Teach/One Assist: One adult delivers instruction while the other adult circulates around the room to provide assistance to individuals or small groups of students.

Team Teaching: Both adults are actively involved in teaching and play off each other during instruction.

Parallel Teaching: The class is split into two flexible heterogeneous groups. Each adult leads a group and covers the same content using the same instructional strategies.

Station Teaching: Center-based teaching in which each adult leads a different group. Students are doing different activities.

Alternative Teaching: One adult leads a large group of students while the other adult leads a smaller group. The small group can pursue a variety of activities, including but not limited to enrichment for students who are ahead, remediation for students who need re-teaching, and pre-teaching for specific students.

Complementary Teaching: One adult does something to enhance the instruction provided by the other adult (e.g., paraphrases statements, models note-taking on the active board, directs focus to technical vocabulary for the content area, demonstrates use of mnemonic devices for studying).

(Adapted from Friend & Cook, 2012)

The Level 3 feedback in Table 7.6 correctly identifies the co-teaching model as Alternative Teaching. However, a shallow understanding affects the feedback: "where one group is smaller than the other." All unequal

Table 7.6 Level 3 Feedback and Something Better

Level 3 Feedback	Better Iteration
Students were in two groups: six students at the kidney table and the rest in their desks facing the whiteboard. It is clear from the grouping that *Alternative Teaching was being used, where one group is smaller than the other.*	Students were in two groups: six students at the kidney table and the rest in their desks facing the whiteboard. The larger group listened to the first 2:30 minutes of a Khan Academy video about dividing fractions. Following this clip, students were partnered up and asked to solve one problem in multiple ways.

The group at the kidney table also turned to watch the video; however, following the video, all students were given Cuisenaire rods and one problem to model. "As you work, please pretend your brain has a volume control. When I touch the red dot in front of you, take the mute off so I can hear what's going on in your head." As each student spoke, notes were taken on individual sticky notes that were placed in manila folders.

The Alternative Teaching model used today presented six students a concrete lesson requiring manipulatives. The lesson plan indicated that these students had exhibited misconceptions on the most recent assessment. |

groupings in co-teaching situations are not automatically the Alternative Teaching model. In addition, the feedback simply lists the model, not providing any fodder so the teachers may consider their co-teaching model choice for this observation as well as their future choices.

Just like the beginning of their own teacher evaluation journey, Decatur leaders first focused on *identifying* without attempting to integrate interpretation or evaluation of the seven models. This is analogous to Decatur's second year when leaders checked boxes on a checklist, refraining from narrative feedback.

It became quite clear through the leadership co-teaching study that teachers did not share the same language around co-teaching. The special education department, which had been integrated into the teacher quality professional development the entire time, spearheaded a year-long study of the models with teachers of students with disabilities. The final group to be added included general education co-teachers.

Some schools embraced the models and saw their utility in other settings. Early Intervention Program (remedial) teachers began planning with the models in mind when they provided push-in support. English Language Learner inclusion support was also considered at some places.

As with so many situations in education, monetary pressures prompted an important change. The primary schools each included a significant number of paraprofessionals in their staffing plans. Besides paraprofessionals to support some students with disabilities, regular education teachers also shared the services of individuals who engaged in a host of tasks ranging from student monitoring to completing required paperwork to small group instruction and conferencing.

Combined with this budget pressure and learning about co-teaching was the required implementation of Response to Intervention (RtI) in Georgia. RtI certainly is deserving of its own set of innovation configuration maps and process story. However, the germane connection here is the necessary conversations about what constitutes an intervention and who provides them. In an attempt to be very clear about the role of certain staff members, Decatur moved to the labels of "intervention teacher" and "intervention paraprofessional." This also helped Decatur become more flexible about scheduling and student assignment: intervention teachers, if properly certified, could support students at multiple tiers.

Why this matters for writing high-quality feedback is this: a greater percentage of classrooms now have the potential of co-teaching situations.

Any time more than one adult is in the room, an opportunity for co-teaching exists. This new reality created urgency among leaders to gain more fluency with the co-teaching models.

Level 2 Feedback

Leaders who can produce Level 2 feedback (Table 7.7) often use their descriptive skills but lack the consistency to identify the model.

The Level 2 feedback in Table 7.8 paints a clear picture of the moves this co-teaching pair made to support their students' mathematical learning. Grouping based on assessment results is a worthwhile strategy with proven results, but the thinking of the teacher is still unclear. The italicized text in the better iteration creates a value-add about purpose: Were the observed instructional moves and decisions intentional? Did the observed teacher intentionally choose to change the order of across and down for her group? Was the commutative property an impromptu reference?

Some leaders moved right from Level 3 to Level 1 as they focused on co-teaching. However, there were some that still had difficulty with model identification. Some of these leaders had the capacity to provide rich

Table 7.7 Co-Teaching Model: Level 2 Feedback

	1	2	3	4
Co-Teaching Model *Purpose:* to identify purposes and jobs of multiple adults in classrooms		In co-teaching situations, feedback is **related** to the co-teaching model(s) used but the model is not identified. *"Ms. Smith drew a Tree Map on the whiteboard as you discussed with students."*	In co-teaching situations, the co-teaching model(s) is identified but **disconnected** from any feedback. *"Today's lesson used the Complementary Co-Teaching model."*	In co-teaching situations, **nothing** in the feedback **reflects on the reality** of multiple adults present in the classroom. *[Feedback does not reference multiple adults in the classroom.]*

Table 7.8 Level 2 Feedback and Something Better

Level 2 Feedback	Better Iteration
"So, kids, even though we are in just-right math groups, we watched you work yesterday and noticed some things. In just a moment, I will call some names to work with Mr. Lamont and some to work with me." Observation was used as an assessment strategy to formatively check learning and plan appropriate activities for the two groups. Students in Mr. Lamont's group created arrays using manipulatives. The verbal directions were consistently given as across first, down second. Students in your group also created arrays using manipulatives, but directions were sometimes given with across first, other times down first. After each array, the number sentence was modeled on a small whiteboard. Toward the end in your group, explicit connections were made to the commutative property: "Who remembers what it is called in math when the order of numbers can be changed?"	"So, kids, even though we are in just-right math groups, we watched you work yesterday and noticed some things. In just a moment, I will call some names to work with Mr. Lamont and some to work with me." Observation was used as an assessment strategy to formatively check learning and plan appropriate activities for the two groups. Students in Mr. Lamont's group created arrays using manipulatives. The verbal directions were consistently given as across first, down second. Students in your group also created arrays using manipulatives, but directions were sometimes given with across first, other times down first. After each array, the number sentence was modeled on a small whiteboard. Toward the end in your group, explicit connections were made to the commutative property: "Who remembers what it is called in math when the order of numbers can be changed?" *Based on the students' responses in both groups, it appears that the instructional choices in both groups matched the need of the students. It is unclear if the co-teaching model was intended to be Parallel Teaching or Alternative Teaching. The lesson plans did not indicate if the instructional moves in each group would be different or not: "Split students into groups based on the assessment results."*

description about what was occurring in classrooms with both adults and could articulate the impacts of these planning and teaching decisions for students. Although this was a small percentage of leaders in that district, it was important to denote this behavior on the Innovation Configuration Map because it represented an unacceptable variation.

A leader who exhibits Level 2 feedback is able to capture the teaching and learning work of multiple adults in a classroom. The observer can both document interactions and draw connections and limitations from the dance of the two adults. Notice the last phrase did not say: "from the dance of the two co-teachers." As part of their instrumental knowing and learning, Decatur leaders agreed to not label co-teaching unless it met the criteria of one of the adopted models.

The language of "co-teaching" had become part of the vernacular, part of the very furniture (think the lyrics of "Consider Yourself" from the musical *Oliver:* "Consider yourself at home! Consider yourself part of the furniture."). Just like in our dwellings, we sometimes take the furniture for granted—the placement, the feel, the look. Labeling the practices of two adults in a classroom as co-teaching was the accepted norm. It was necessary to surface and question that assumption in order to build our instrumental knowing about what constituted co-teaching and what did not.

This context made it extremely important for observers to use their new vocabulary whenever possible, especially in written observations. Just like young children acquiring vocabulary, using the words frequently is important.

I became acutely aware of this through my older son, Addison. At a certain point in both our lives, I frequently brought him to school and would take phone calls in the car. Sometimes these calls would involve coaching other colleagues, possibly in searching for a protocol to match their purpose or mediating their thinking about a particular issue. One day as we approached his school, he requested technology (specifically iPad) time during the school week as opposed to just weekends. As he verbally constructed his case he ended with, "And an assumption you hold is that more technology is a bad thing."

As I bit my lower lip to prevent a substantial smile, I peered into the rear view mirror and said, "You might be right about that assumption. But more importantly, an assumption you might hold is that I am willing to change my mind." An immediate scowl from him, followed by my long-arm reach back to tickle his knee, ended the conversation as we turned into the carpool lane.

Not only did Addison nail his use of "assumption," he knew me well enough (apparently from listening to my conversation input on the phone calls) to use that vocabulary in his persuasive attempt. That same attention to language builds a stronger belief in co-teaching partnerships and observers that we might be saying the same thing.

As we discovered in Chapter 1, one reason Decatur chose innovation configuration maps as the evaluation structure was the ability to set expectations on each desired outcome and identify each possible variation. The shading of cells represents unacceptable variations and a prompt for leaders to prioritize that desired outcome in their own practice.

Shading can change over time as the group determines. This desired outcome may be a perfect example of an expectation that increases over time. If studying the co-teaching models and identifying them in practice is a growing edge for a group, it may be apropos to only shade Level 4 at the onset of the learning.

In the first iteration of the High-Quality Feedback Innovation Configuration Map, no items about co-teaching existed. The first modification was to add a desired outcome about the co-teaching models. As with any addition, the need stemmed from data collected from the group: through written reflections at the end of each professional development session and from the written observational feedback we produced at each meeting.

A very intriguing pronoun use began to emerge as written feedback was analyzed. Language use from the observers indicated assumed power dynamics between the two adults in classrooms (Table 7.9). Although the group had agreed on the desired outcome of point of view (Chapter 5), old habits crept in, especially when considering co-teaching situations. Another desired outcome related to co-teaching was needed. Consider the Level 2 feedback example in Table 7.10.

Table 7.10 is rated as Level 2 feedback for co-teaching model in that the actions of both adults are mentioned but the possible co-teaching model is not identified.

Table 7.9 Co-Teaching Equity: Level 2 Feedback

	1	2	3	4
Co-Teaching Equity *Purpose:* to not reinforce hierarchies between adults		In co-teaching situations, language suggests **power:** "having" another colleague do something. *"Consider having your co-teacher alternatively teach during your mini-lesson."*		

Table 7.10 Level 2 Feedback and Something Better

Level 2 Feedback	Better Iteration
Students were given the opportunity to work on their chemical equation project either independently or in groups. As students made their choices, both adults circulated to check-in.	Students were given the opportunity to work on their chemical equation project either independently or in groups. As students made their choices, both adults circulated to check-in.
Consider having your co-teacher pull a small group during that time so those students can voice their plans, similar to the verbal rehearsal before writing in an ELA class.	It is unclear which co-teaching model today's lesson demonstrates. Based on the nine minutes it took for some students to begin working (some identified with a disability, some not), it appears that some students might have benefited from a brief conversation about their plan, similar to the verbal rehearsal before writing in an ELA class. This Alternative Teaching co-teaching model could work quite well for this situation.

Regarding co-teaching equity, this excerpt also is rated as Level 2. The italicized phrase in the Level 2 feedback is problematic: "having your co-teacher." This language connotes power and hierarchy, as if the regular education teacher has sole decision-making responsibility for the students in that room, and through that default also controls the other adult, the other co-teacher.

The better iteration in Table 7.10 first frames the assumption about the co-teaching model (or lack thereof): "It is unclear which co-teaching model today's lesson demonstrates." Following that important line, the second assumption uses conditional language so the teacher could ponder this potential gap.

It isn't as simple as avoiding a pronoun. Other language can still exist that clearly denotes a power relationship. Notice the change in the italicized text in Table 7.11.

Removing the pronoun is not the magic elixir to attain co-teaching equity. It truly takes a re-consideration of how often we use ownership language in our practice of crafting written feedback. In Table 7.12 are two versions where we are more careful about power dynamics in our written language.

Table 7.11 Pronoun Changes for Equity

Version 1	Version 2
Consider having your co-teacher pull a small group during that time so those students can voice their plans, similar to the verbal rehearsal before writing in an ELA class.	*Consider having Mrs. Barnes* pull a small group during that time so those students can voice their plans, similar to the verbal rehearsal before writing in an ELA class.

Table 7.12 Consideration of Power Dynamics

Version 1	Version 2
It is unclear which co-teaching model today's lesson demonstrates. Based on the nine minutes it took for some students to begin working (some identified with a disability, some not), it appears that some students might have benefited from a brief conversation about their plan, similar to the verbal rehearsal before writing in an ELA class. This Alternative Teaching co-teaching model could work quite well for this situation.	Consider how one adult might address a persistent need of the group: students who consistently demonstrate difficulty in starting projects. A small group convened during that time could involve students who might voice their plans aloud, similar to the verbal rehearsal before writing in an ELA class.

Level 1 Feedback

Identifying the co-teaching model of an observation is not enough (Table 7.13). The models become truly useful when the observer weaves together the lesson content and instructional moves.

Consider your own setting if you are in a school, or the last school where you worked. Create a pie chart representing the percentage of co-teaching models that are used when co-teaching actually is occurring. For instance, Figure 7.1 might represent a particular school.

Why might this be the case? What might be the root causes of this picture? As a leadership team discusses, the following could be sample responses:

- We included all the kindergarten paraprofessionals in our percentages. They are mostly assisting all day.
- One Teach, One Observe is tempting to include in our data set, but when we consider the definition of what the observer does ("conducts

Table 7.13 Desired Outcomes: Co-Teaching Model and Co-Teaching Equity

	1	2	3	4
Co-Teaching Model *Purpose:* to identify purposes and jobs of multiple adults in classrooms	In co-teaching situations, the identified co-teaching model(s) serves as a **foundation** for the feedback. *"The Tree Map drawn on the board by Ms. Smith as complementary co-teaching while you were discussing was referenced three times by students later in the discussion."*	In co-teaching situations, feedback is **related** to the co-teaching model(s) used but the model is not identified. *"Ms. Smith drew a Tree Map on the whiteboard as you discussed with students."*	In co-teaching situations, the co-teaching model(s) is identified but **disconnected** from any feedback. *"Today's lesson used the Complementary Co-Teaching model."*	In co-teaching situations, **nothing** in the feedback **reflects on the reality of** multiple adults present in the classroom. *[Feedback does not reference multiple adults in the classroom.]*
Co-Teaching Equity *Purpose:* to not reinforce hierarchies between adults	In co-teaching situations, language focuses on **equity:** on the **action** rather than the person. *"One Teach, One Observe was used. This content seems to need a co-teaching model where both adults are more actively engaged with students."*	In co-teaching situations, language suggests **power:** "having" another colleague do something. *"Consider having your co-teacher alternatively teach during your mini-lesson."*		

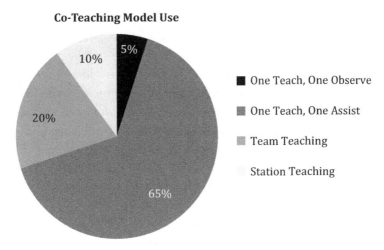

Co-Teaching Model Use

- One Teach, One Observe
- One Teach, One Assist
- Team Teaching
- Station Teaching

Figure 7.1 Sample School's Co-Teaching Model Use

systematic observation of students to gather meaningful data"), we decided that we never see it.

- We see some grouping that looks like Parallel Teaching, with similar-sized groups and the same content, but the teachers are not using the same strategies.
- We never see Complementary Teaching. Perhaps our colleagues think that if one person is primarily teaching, they need to either silently assist with student behaviors or speak up, peppering in their perspectives as Team Teachers do. They might not even know another option could exist in these situations.
- Lack of common grade level or department planning on our block schedule between both members of co-teaching teams causes them to default to One Teach, One Assist or Team Teaching.

A significant assumption that undergirds conversations about co-teaching models is this: *Observers assume that a decision was made about which co-teaching model will be used.* The decision-making process in planning for co-teaching experiences may be the most important lynchpin your feedback can provide.

Consider this feedback offered in a high school co-teaching situation:

It is unclear about the decision-making process that resulted in Parallel Teaching for today. References were made to "quiz scores" and "plug some holes" as students were placed in groups with two adults. Both groups used the same materials and same processes with their smaller group. Despite the smaller numbers, 3–5 students dominated each of the two discussions about inert gases, never once answering a question incorrectly. If the quiz data matches the observational data collected during the discussion, this may have been an opportunity to use Alternative Teaching, supporting groups of students with different needs.

Or here's another example that builds on previous observations to make a point:

One Teach, One Assist was used as students engaged in a simulation about the Civil War. All material was shared orally by one adult as the other circulated and checked in with student groups.

During this school year, each observation of this co-taught class has noted One Teach, One Assist. Although possible, it is improbable that the student content addressed during each observation lent itself best to this model, which is one of the least active co-teaching models. Please determine a time when other models can be observed and be prepared to provide evidence of why that model was chosen for those learners for that content on that day.

A Note Re: "You"

You may have noticed the use of "you" in several examples in this chapter and are wondering how that fits with expectations laid out in Chapter 5: Why Point of View Is Significant. It still is ideal when passive voice can be primarily used, avoiding "you," "I," "the teacher," or "Mrs. Johnson." However, when describing an interaction between two adults in a classroom it is sometimes difficult to describe students, as they might be responding to a particular adult rather than the co-teaching team. As you explore how to write feedback for co-teaching situations, grant yourself a temporary reprieve from point of view until you feel more fluent in using various models as the underpinning for productive feedback.

Putting It All Together

Table 7.14 High-Quality Feedback Innovation Configuration Map

	1	2	3	4
Description *Purpose:* to see and hear what's going on in a classroom	Feedback is highly **descriptive**, balancing rich descriptions of student behaviors and teacher behaviors. Feedback includes **data** that was seen and heard, using direct **quotations** when appropriate. *"Three students put their heads down during the 10-minute movie, near the 6-minute mark. You remained at the back of the room speaking once to a student. It appeared that 10 students wrote something down. One student near the door used a Flow Map."*	Feedback is mostly **descriptive**, including **approximations** for what was seen and/or heard. Feedback may include student behaviors as well as teacher behaviors. *"Three students slept during the 10-minute movie. You remained at the back of the room watching the movie with the students."*	Feedback uses primarily **evaluative** and **interpretive** language. Feedback may include student behaviors as well as teacher behaviors. *"Students appeared off-task and bored during the movie despite your directions for them to take notes."*	Feedback primarily draws on **evaluative** language. Feedback is limited to teacher behaviors. *"You allowed the sleeping students too long before you intervened."*

(Continued)

Table 7.14 (Continued)

	1	2	3	4
Conditional Language *Purpose:* to ponder a possible gap in practice	Conditional language is effectively used to help the reader **deeply consider gaps** or unintended results. *"At least three standards in this observation seem to be affected by students' responsibilities when they arrive to class."*	Conditional language is effectively used that would spur the reader to **pause and consider.** *"It seems that there may be a connection between instructional time and classroom routines."*	Conditional language is used to offer **suggestions.** *"We are curious about the potential if students had a consistent routine every time they entered their room."*	**Rhetorical questions** are used to suggest. *"What might happen if you had something up on the interactive whiteboard the first moment students entered the room?"*
Point of View *Purpose:* to accept the feedback more about practice than the person	Feedback primarily focuses on **actions** instead of the teacher. Passive voice pervades the feedback. *"The ACTIVBoard was used to model the Circle Map."*	Feedback is primarily written focusing on the **observer.** *"I observed that the ACTIVBoard was used to model the Circle Map."*	Feedback is primarily written from **another person's** point of view. *"**You** used the ACTIVBoard to model the Circle Map."* *"**The teacher** used the ACTIVBoard to model the Circle Map."* *"**Ms. Smith** used the ACTIVBoard to model the Circle Map."*	

Assumptions *Purpose:* to acknowledge the observer has a partial picture	Assumptions inherent in the feedback are **explicitly** identified. *"Students identified that group composition sometimes changes. The grouping rationale today was difficult to ascertain."*	Assumptions are drawn from observational evidence. The assumptions are **not recognized** nor identified by the observer. *"Flexible groups are used to offer students more opportunities to learn with others."*	Assumptions are drawn from the **lack of observational evidence.** The assumptions are not recognized nor identified by the observer. *"Consider having the groups organized in more intentional ways based on assessment."*	
Co-Teaching Model *Purpose:* to identify purposes and jobs of multiple adults in classrooms	In co-teaching situations, the identified co-teaching model(s) serves as a **foundation** for the feedback. *"The Tree Map drawn on the board by Ms. Smith as complementary co-teaching while you were discussing was referenced three times by students later in the discussion."*	In co-teaching situations, feedback is **related** to the co-teaching model(s) used but the model is not identified. *"Ms. Smith drew a Tree Map on the whiteboard as you discussed with students."*	In co-teaching situations, the co-teaching model(s) is identified but **disconnected** from any feedback. *"Today's lesson used the Complementary Co-Teaching model."*	In co-teaching situations, **nothing** in the feedback **reflects on the reality of** multiple adults present in the classroom. *[Feedback does not reference multiple adults in the classroom.]*

(Continued)

Table 7.14 (Continued)

	1	2	3	4
Co-Teaching Equity *Purpose:* to not reinforce hierarchies between adults	In co-teaching situations, language focuses on **equity:** on the **action** rather than the person. *"One Teach, One Observe was used. This content seems to need a co-teaching model where both adults are more actively engaged with students."*	In co-teaching situations, language suggests **power:** "having" another colleague do something. *"Consider having your co-teacher alternatively teach during your mini-lesson."*		

Accurate descriptions of classrooms, gracious doses of conditional language, a consistent point of view that emphasizes passive voice, and clearly articulated assumptions create successful conditions for the reader, the teacher, to sound like this:

- *Acknowledgement. The more you see and hear, the better I can analyze why those things are happening in my room.*

- *Respect. I have enough lists in my life—at work and at home. I appreciate being able to read feedback where I can decide what to add to or integrate into my list.*

- *Distance. I want to let go of my classroom sometime, to not think about it 24/7, but it's hard. Reading feedback like this helps me step away, albeit temporarily.*

- *Community. Sometimes you get things wrong, but at least it is clear where you are taking a leap and where you have the evidence to back it up.*

Combined with the following two specific desired outcomes in co-teaching situations, teachers are successfully positioned to auto-supervise:

- *Purpose. Shared definitions about co-teaching models ensure that you, me, and my co-teaching partner are all saying and meaning the same thing.*

- *Equity. I don't like being "had" by anyone and don't want to think about "having" my co-teaching partner do anything either. Saying "partner" really matters to me.*

Here is a sample of Level 1 feedback for all six desired outcomes:

Students moved to the rug to hear the second reading of *Push! Pull! Go!* Specific vocabulary was reinforced using PAT: point, act out, and tell. In an approximate breakdown, "tell" is used over 50% of the time.

During the read-aloud, Ms. Williams sat near the group with a clipboard, collecting behavior data on two students.

A phone's timer was used to end the data collection; the rest of the read-aloud spent sitting on the floor as part of the back row. This One Teach, One Observe was a fluid model use and did not require any time away from students.

A phonological rhythmic chant was used to dismiss each row back to their tables. The transition took less than 25 seconds for all 22 five-year-olds to sit.

"For math workshop today, only one area has been changed: geoboards. After we explored these yesterday, we added them because you know what to do with them and what not to do with them. Give a signal if you remember one of the 'don'ts' with geoboards." Multiple students raised their hands and several were called on, with each answer being repeated aloud. After five behaviors either to do or not to do were voiced, students were called who would start math time in small groups with an adult. Daily 5 literacy time is a smooth, drama-free time in this classroom. An assumption that could be present with literacy time is that the repetition and demonstration of behaviors (both what to do and what not to do) made a significant difference on the pleasant culture during that time of the day. That productive modeling (often by students) could be lifted and applied when new math manipulatives are introduced to workshop.

Once the chime was rung, students bustled to either their small group or an area of choice, replete with a math journal that included a spot where each student documented their first activity choice during math workshop.

Students in one group were patterning 2-D shapes (square, circle, triangle, hexagon). Each pattern was generated by the adult verbally and demonstrated by the students.

T: "Square, circle, square, circle."

T: "This time it's going to be trickier. Four sides, three sides, four sides, three sides."

T: "How might we label the patterns we have done thus far?"

S: "ABABABABABAB . . ."

T: [interrupting] "Yes, Abdul, it's ABAB, and you certainly are remembering that patterns are infinite! Here's another . . ."

The other group was using pattern blocks to engage in open sorts, creating groups of their own attributes.

T: "That pile looks interesting. What makes all of those pieces go together?"

S: "They all have a flat side."

T: "Hmmm . . . I'm curious how big that pile will be in a bit."

Based on a reporting sheet seen on a clipboard, every group is seen by both adults over the course of two days. The choice of Station Teaching allows each adult to give immediate and direct feedback to each student in small group.

Students referred to both adults by Ms. and their last name. When asked, 'who is your teacher?' each of four students said, "Ms. Tatnall . . . and Ms. Monroe, too." One student did add after a few second pause, "Ms. Monroe is our para, ya' know." Two co-teaching models were effectively used during this observation.

Fifteen minutes was spent in the classroom diligently collecting description, followed by 10 minutes of adding any interpretation and evaluation. Twenty-five minutes later, this feedback was sent to this teacher who is now successfully positioned to autosupervise.

Try It Yourself

1. Consider how possessive language may have infiltrated your language as a leader. Ask a trusted colleague to listen for the following phrases: "my teachers," "my school," "my students." Brainstorm with others what other language choices could be substituted for these phrases and what those changes might net for yourself and your school community.

2. Make a pie chart of the co-teaching practices in your school for yourself. Compare with other observers. Finally, ask co-teaching

pairs to each independently make a pie chart of their co-teaching class. Consider convening a short meeting for the pair to unveil their pie charts to each other.

3. Look at an upcoming faculty meeting agenda and ask yourself, "How might I model co-teaching in this agenda without making the content about co-teaching?" Choose an agenda item whose content could benefit from a co-teaching model and ask someone (e.g., teacher, assistant principal, a principal colleague from another school) to plan with you. After the experience is over, ask the faculty to debrief how it went to have a co-teacher/co-facilitator during that part of the agenda and what value-add it may have provided. Be sure to explicitly voice the model name.

4. Convene a group of co-teaching pairs and interview them about their planning practices:

   How do you make time for co-teaching planning?

   What do you plan first—the model or the content? Do you have a "go-to" model? If so, what is it?

5. Refute this statement: "All co-teachers are Team Teachers."

6. Consider your learning from this chapter: What practices from this chapter are 10-degree changes? Which might require a 90-degree change in your practice? What might be first on your docket?

Reference List

Breidenstein, A., Fahey, K., Glickman, C., & Hensley, F. (2012). *Leading for powerful learning: A guide for instructional leaders.* New York, NY: Teacher's College Press.

Friend, M., & Cook, L. (2012). *Interactions: Collaboration skills for school professionals.* New York, NY: Pearson.

8

Nurturing a Culture of Feedback

Language matters. In Chapter 2, I posed the unfortunate reality of school leaders dedicating significant time and energy creating evaluation narratives that do not cause thinking. Very well-intentioned leaders search for the "just-right" phrases to deliver difficult or tricky messages. They long for the comment banks of old and when those aren't made publicly available, they create their own personal repositories or collaboratively build a covert cache with a few respected others.

Sometimes these leaders believe that writing a meaningful teacher evaluation narrative is not a skill to develop; rather, it is a task to be accomplished, hopefully causing one of the desired results in the feedback reader, the teacher:

1. Feeling *good:* a positive "stroke"
2. Feeling *worried:* a clear understanding that she/he is in trouble
3. Feeling *panicky:* a desire to resign before termination

Notice none of the desired outcomes include any of the following for the feedback reader, the teacher:

1. Feeling *excited:* another set of data reinforcing what she/he thought was true in the classroom
2. Feeling *reflective:* wondering about an assumption raised in the feedback

3. Feeling *focused:* someone noticed what I've really been working on and I can now move my energy to something else

Consistently using the desired outcomes outlined in Chapters 3–6—

*   Description
*   Conditional language
*   Consistent point of view
*   Explicit assumptions

—in written feedback produces teachers who appreciate, even long for, high-quality written feedback. Meeting the desires of teachers builds school culture.

Barriers

Even after studying each of these desired outcomes throughout this book, you may still be stuck thinking about implementation. This next section discusses a few common barriers to crafting feedback in this way and for these purposes.

I Don't Have Time

Like with most developed skills, fluency is not immediate, but it is worth the commitment to persevere. For leaders who have consistently summarized 30-minute observations into a few sentences or a paragraph, writing descriptive feedback seems like a big lift.

Before this becomes the main or solitary reason for abandoning your development in constructing high-quality written feedback, try it for two weeks. Use the time to build fluency in what happens *in* the classroom, holding yourself accountable for describing 100% of the time in the classroom, using the time following the observation to add any interpretation or evaluation you deem necessary, resulting in no more than 20% interpretation or evaluation (Figure 8.1).

At the conclusions of Chapters 4–7, complete evaluation narratives are included, along with the time taken to craft those records. Just like an

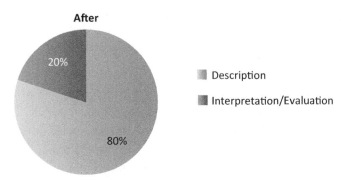

Figure 8.1 Post-Observation Focus

Table 8.1 Feedback Regimen

Day	Observation	Minutes Spent in Observation	Minutes Spent After Observation	Total Time
Monday **Week One**	#1	5	10	15
Tuesday **Week One**	#2	5	10	15
Wednesday **Week One**	#3, #4	5	10	30
Thursday **Week One**	#5	10	15	25
Friday **Week One**	Read through all narratives and gather feedback on your feedback.			
Monday **Week Two**	#6, #7	10	15	50
Tuesday **Week Two**	#8	15	20	35
Wednesday **Week Two**	#9	15	15	30
Thursday **Week Two**	#10, #11	15	15	60
Friday **Week Two**	Read through #6–11 narratives and gather feedback on your feedback.			

exercise regimen starts slowly and increases, Table 8.1 is a two-week sequence you might use as you develop.

I suspect that adding up this total time (4 hours, 20 minutes) without implementing the desired outcomes from the High-Quality Feedback Innovation Configuration Map will not yield 11 complete narratives teachers would find helpful and supportive of their growth.

Leaders I coach are indebted to timers! The parameter causes a prioritizing that many leaders do practice the discipline to organically implement. The timer is certainly helpful in a classroom, but it is more important for the column called "Time Spent After Observation."

Teachers at My School Need More Direction Than Just Description

Two concerns with this barrier: one a practical matter, one an assumption. Practically speaking, although description is the lion's share of high-quality feedback narratives (~80%), it is not the sole ingredient. The purpose of using descriptive language is clear: to see and hear what's going on in a classroom. From that objective foundation, the feedback can take multiple directions, as demonstrated numerous times in this book.

An assumption the speaker of this barrier may hold is that teachers in his school are not reflective about their classrooms. A similar assumption is often held for new teachers and operationalized vis-à-vis highly structured induction programs. These sorts of well-meaning experiences assume all teachers new to the profession need the same scope and sequence of topics: classroom management, report cards, parent teacher conferences, the teacher evaluation system. I found a significantly different need with a group of novice teachers. Their most common needs were around assessment, grading, and relationships with colleagues (Van Soelen, 2003).

Teacher reflection does not necessarily have a directly proportionate relationship with years in the profession. A teacher quite new to the profession may hungrily receive descriptive feedback, anxious to compare an observer's view of her classroom with her own. If all she receives are more ways to manage her room, phrase her mini-lesson, or re-direct student misbehaviors, she stagnates in Conscious Incompetence—certainly not where we desire our teaching staff to take root.

In Chapter 3, we used the tool of paraphrasing, expertly leveraged by cognitive coaches. If someone said to me in person, "Teachers at my school need more direction than just description," I might paraphrase in response: "So an assumption you hold is that you need to do most of the thinking for the people with whom you work."

Kegan's constructive-developmental theory of knowing was summarized in Table 7.4, used as a reference point in a decision made about how to proceed with learning about co-teaching. Ellie Drago-Severson and Jessica Blum-DeStefano (2014) have considered Kegan's theory in posing a developmental approach to giving feedback to teachers. They believe a teacher's developmental stage is an important consideration in crafting feedback. For instrumental knowers, the authors summarize their need as "Tell me what I need to do" (p. 18). For self-transforming knowers, the catch line is "We can figure this out together" (p. 20).

This view of categorizing adults can be dangerous if used in generalities or in extremes. For instance, a principal may erroneously assume that a teacher new to the profession is automatically an instrumental knower. Or a well-intentioned assistant principal may believe a teacher is a socializing knower as a teacher of literacy but doesn't consider that her way of knowing may be different when she is discussing mathematics.

Every teacher is deserving of rich description that creates a platform for thinking. When teacher evaluation narratives are idea-heavy or compliment-rich, the reader of the feedback, the teacher, has very little to think about. The teacher might evaluate the plausibility of the suggestions, but that's about it. Conversely, teacher evaluation narratives solidly grounded in description create the conditions for educators, for professionals, to think.

Teachers at My School Are Quite Good—They Have Way More Expertise Than I Do

How exciting is that?! You might be tempted to forgo observations, thinking that expert teachers need leaders to just leave them alone. Resist that urge and remember the Passover metaphor from Chapter 1: When you taught, were you that classroom your school leader "passed over" because you had all your ducks in a row? Just because you didn't have rich feedback to improve your teaching craft does not mean others do not want it, need it, or deserve it.

Take yourself out of the past and think about your work right now. Teachers are unique because observation is a driving force in their performance management system. Imagine if that was true for being a school leader—what if someone collected high-quality feedback for you during a staff meeting? A parent Q and A session? An IEP meeting? A teacher coaching session? A professional development session you are leading? A leadership team meeting? You would want the same high-quality feedback you are trying to integrate into the feedback you write for teachers.

Teacher Evaluation Really Isn't Our Avenue for Growth—That Is What We Use Walkthroughs For

Remember the continuum from Chapter 2 represented here as Figure 8.2?

There is a playful activity I sometimes use with groups called *Say, Say, Do* (http://schoolreforminitiative.org/doc/say_say_do.pdf). A group attempts to successfully perform a task that grows in complexity. Starting in a circle, a facilitator calls out one of four directions: Step In, Step Out, Step Right, Step Left. These can be called out in any sequence and directions can be repeated. In the first round, called "Say, Say, Do," the facilitator will say a command and the group will repeat it back and do it at the same time. After 30–45 seconds of this fun, kinesthetic experience, the group stops and reflects on their work thus far.

Time for Round 2: Say, Say, Do Opposite. Whatever command the facilitator gives, the group repeats it but does the opposite at the same time. As you might suspect, this challenge plays havoc with the brain and groups enjoy their inability to follow such basic directions. After a period of time (and many, many mistakes), the group stops and reflects on their strategies and how they handled the task.

Figure 8.2 Continuum Dialogue Poles

Little do they know there is another round: Say, Say Opposite, Do! Whatever command the facilitator gives, the group repeats the opposite, but then physically completes the original command. Groups often experience more cognitive challenge and laugh to mitigate their mistakes. Finally, relieved there is no Round 4, the group debriefs the whole experience, sometimes from the vantage point of working in efficient and effective ways.

The lack of congruence between actions and words makes Rounds 2 and 3 difficult. We don't want to intentionally cause this mismatch that requires so much cognitive energy to overcome. It is akin to a parent telling a young child that sometimes it matters holding her hand in a parking lot and other times not. The inconsistency of the message makes it quite difficult for the child to construct his or her meaning.

However, we might be doing exactly that when it comes to the practices of teacher evaluation and walkthroughs:

- Wednesday: "Don't worry, Ms. Jones, these are just walkthroughs—collecting feedback for the whole school."
- Friday: "So, Ms. Jones, today it matters if your students are really learning and can identify their goals because I'm using the district teacher evaluation form."

What makes Wednesday any different of a learning day for a student than Friday? Why would the teacher's learning matter more during one observation than another?

Just like Round 1 in the activity just described, it is easier to match words and actions (Say = Do). Schools where frequent observations occur that always matter for the teacher's learning report less stress about observations. If you've frequently video recorded yourself doing anything (singing, teaching, playing a sport), you know when it became second nature to have the video running—you finally moved past the "other eyes and ears" and focused on the task at hand.

When a school becomes a place where meaningful feedback is frequently given and received, teacher evaluation is the norm, not the anomaly. Twenty-eight percent of human resources professionals believe supervisors are only completing forms (Stone & Heen, 2014). Not so in schools where leaders efficiently and effectively craft high-quality written feedback.

I Think It Is Better to Offer Feedback Orally with Teachers—It's Too Intimidating in Writing

This final barrier certainly has merit: I concur that in many places written feedback feels weightier than a conversation. In fact, some leaders use written feedback only in situations where they are trying to document (e.g., an email following up after a conference with a teacher). The writing does not make it scary: it is the *use* and *frequency* of the writing that creates the conditions that may feel scary.

Kim Marshall (2009) lobbies for an oral approach to feedback. Approximately 7–10 "mini-observations" are conducted in lieu of longer classroom observations. After each mini-observation, an in-person discussion occurs between observer and the observed, focusing on *one* concept, behavior, or moment. Marshall found teachers to be more open to this observation process and appreciated conversations about their practice with their supervisor.

Reflection in schools is highly desired and oftentimes difficult to implement. Teaching frameworks like writing or reading workshops build in time for sharing and reflection, but that specific step is often truncated: "Oh, kids, we don't have time to share today. Please line up for music!"

By utilizing oral conversations about what was seen and heard without any text (e.g., data) provided ahead of time, teachers are forced to reflect immediately—on the spot. I remember an assistant principal, at a school where I taught, who grew frustrated with middle schoolers just before a parent performance. With crisp diction and a clipped tone, she chided them: "Sing now! Be joyful!" In some ways, looking for the random moment to debrief with teachers is saying, "Think now! Be reflective!"

It is similar to feelings generated during job interviews when a question, seemingly out of the blue, disarms us. In those moments, it is truly unclear (notice the desired outcome here: explicit assumption) whether the goal of the question is (1) the answer, or (2) to see how the candidate reacts to a surprising question. In my own interviewing practice I adopt the "let's be clear on what we're assessing" model, thus I always provide the interview questions in writing to candidates 3–5 minutes before they walk in.

In-Person Conferencing

Teachers live frenetic lives, and impromptu conversations about practice may further exacerbate their feelings of not being in control. Marshall's method may have a different goal than the High-Quality Feedback Innovation Configuration Map, which systematically builds more reflective practitioners who can autosupervise and demonstrate Conscious Competence. With this kind of high-quality feedback, a face-to-face conference with the observer is often not necessary.

Even though conferences are often optional, there certainly will be times where the observer or the observed desire to or are required to have conferences. The use of observation narratives that include highly descriptive feedback requires a different approach in these face-to-face interactions.

Although not specifically preparing for a conference with this quality of feedback, Shelly Arneson (2015) notes the introductory error that many leaders make: Even if the administrator has only glowing things to say about a classroom lesson, the postobservation meeting is often one-sided, sounding like this:

> "I thought it was great. I liked the way you grouped the students. Any questions before you sign to acknowledge you received this?" Even if the teacher wanted to talk about the lesson, this type of introduction shuts the door.
>
> (p. 32. Reprinted with permission of the Association for Supervision and Curriculum Development, from *Improving Teaching One Conversation at a Time,* Shelly Arneson, *72*(7), 2015; permission conveyed through Copyright Clearance Center, Inc.)

Lightly drawing on two sources as fodder, the process in Table 8.2 is recommended in a conference where highly descriptive feedback is included. Drawing from Bambrick-Santoyo's (2012) *Leverage Leadership* and a peer observation process called Video Camera (http://schoolreform initiative.org/doc/video_camera.pdf), this process creates a shared experience where both the observed and observer own the responsibility of making sense of the collected data and then create a plan stemming from their discussion.

What sets this procedure apart from others are the first two steps. Stopping to freshly read feedback and then inquire about alignments and gaps creates a

Table 8.2 Face-to-Face Conference Process With High-Quality Written Feedback

Step	Description	Possible Language
1. Read feedback	Both the observed and observer begin the conference by reading the feedback.	*"I suspect you have read this feedback before today, and I certainly have, but I know how busy both of us are. Why don't we just take 3–5 minutes right now to re-read? Then we can make sure we are both clear."*
2. Consider alignments and gaps	This step assumes that observer/observed reliability is not automatic.	*"So now we've both had a chance to read. What seems right on with what you remember about this day and this timeframe?"* *"What is surprising in the feedback or seems like a gap between what you remember and what you now read?"*
3. Choose a gap	Depending on the concern level of the observer, the pair might build consensus on which gap could be mutually explored.	*"It sounds like there are two ideas we have talked about already. Which of the two might be more important for you to work on?"*
4. Create an action step	Identifying a tangible action is crucial toward having a shared understanding once the conference is complete.	*"What might be the first step toward bridging the gap between what we have been talking about and how we want it to be?"*
5. Predict roadblocks and practice	Bambrick-Santoyo (2012) argues the necessity for a rehearsal of any teaching behavior that needs changing.	*"As we both want to make sure we progress on this plan, what might get in the way?"* *"Let's actually try it out right now. How might that go with your students?"*
6. Set timeline	As with any planning process, timeframes provide accountability.	*"When might it make sense that we have completed what we set out with this plan?"* *"Perhaps I could make another visit then the week following— looks like I could schedule it right now."*

common platform that increases the likelihood of a productive conference from that point on. If the feedback has met the threshold of at least 80% description, the observed and observer now have agreement on at least 80% of what was seen and heard—not necessarily what it means (interpretation) or whether something should change in the future (evaluation).

Preparing Staff Members

Whether a teacher is in year one or in year 30, she has at least one written observation narrative to consider when constructing what a "model observation" looks like. This certainly doesn't mean every teacher has experienced high-quality feedback. Instead this phenomenon probably reflects more on the opposite: since many teachers have not experienced high-quality feedback, they have constructed their own model in the absence of any other models to consider.

I suspect the "model observation" for many experienced teachers would include several compliments, a few notations with superlative language (e.g., "best," "model"), and language that almost apologizes for the need to conduct the observation in the first place. This shows the significant gap between what teachers currently experience and what high-quality feedback offers them toward the development of their own practice.

Thus, it is not advisable to spring newly constructed feedback on an unknowing or ill-prepared staff. Just like any instructional or assessment initiative, thoughtful conversations and preparatory work is in order.

1. Be Explicit About Changes You Are Trying to Make in Your Feedback Practice

Although all teachers are not alike and should not be grouped into large generalities, I daresay that as a profession, teachers do not like to be surprised. They have chosen a profession where they are even paid to plan.

We used the table below in Chapter 3, learning about description. Now picture the reader of this feedback, the teacher, if he usually receives the "Before" column from his principal, and now receives the "After" column.

In paper-based evaluation systems, teachers would fret if their written evaluation extended to the back side of a piece of paper. The current

Table 8.3 Before and After

Before	After
Students were on the carpet listening to a nursery rhyme.	There are 20 students sitting on the carpet looking at the poem, "Little Boy Blue," on a colored chart. This nursery rhyme is being used to teach rhyming. The student teacher was sitting on a chair watching instruction.
	Sample responses to students:
	• "We are listening for something that rhymes with horn."
	• "What do you think, E?"
	• When students spoke out loud without being called on: "It's C's turn, let's listen to C."
	Two moments of a formative strategy:
	1. "If you think these two words rhyme, put both hands on your head."
	All students but one put their hands on their head.
	"M, why are both hands on top of your head?"
	Students saw a model of both hands on an adult head.
	2. "If you think that X rhymes with Y, put your pinky on your nose."
	Students saw a model of a pinky on a nose.
	"Why do you have your pinky on your nose? . . . because my pinky is on my nose, so you did it too?"
	One attribute of rhyming words was offered: "Rhyming words are different at the beginning." It is unclear whether this "difference" was about the sound or the actual letter.
	A student added another attribute: "both words have the same sound at the end."

electronic version of this fear is what I heard a teacher say when she logged into her teacher evaluation portal, "Oh, no! I need to scroll down—there's more!"

Principal Derrick Thomas took this charge quite seriously and chose to reverse the roles. After teaching a series of eighth grade math lessons, Derrick showed a video excerpt of his teaching experience to staff and asked them to write high-quality feedback. He used the same electronic tool, Poll Everywhere (http://www.polleverywhere.com), used in his own professional development, so each person's submission was public to each other. Fully admitting it was hard to read the feedback, a more important goal emerged: empathy for feedback writers.

2. Make Sure the Second Observation Happens Quickly

This might seem like an odd piece of advice—thinking about the second observation. What about the first? I contend the first of anything is relatively easy to do and easy to accept. The second makes the expectation more real, with a greater probability of being the new normal.

Kim Marshall (2009) recollects his staff being slow to accept his mini-observations approach, too. However, similar to videotaping, both the teacher and the students grow accustomed to the practice and eventually accept it as the way we do business.

3. Expect and Plan for Resistance

Stone and Heen (2014), Harvard lawyers who authored a specific framework for feedback conversations, realized that intense development for leaders can and does pay dividends, but the feedback loop includes the person receiving the feedback.

Regardless of whether the feedback is delivered in person or through writing, it is difficult to separate the creator of the feedback from the feedback itself. So these authors offer a framework for supervisors to prepare their staff to productively receive feedback. Part of that preparation involves building awareness about triggers that surface when feedback is offered: truth, relationship, and identity. As you examine these three triggers, you will notice that the skills we have been developing in Chapters 3–7 clearly combat the first two triggers.

Truth triggers are set off by the content of the feedback: it is misconstrued, unhelpful, or just plain untrue. If the desired outcome of descriptive language (Chapter 3) is demonstrated well by observers, this feedback trigger is rendered virtually moot.

Relationship triggers are initiated when the interactions between feedback writer and reader adversely affect how the reader interprets the content. Sometimes credibility is questioned *(Really? You think you can tell me about teaching five-year-olds?)*; other times, unrelated exchanges lead to generalization (*I stepped up as department head when no one else would, and now she gives me this feedback?*). The desired outcomes of conditional language (Chapter 4) and assumptions (Chapter 6) curb the credibility concerns, while the desired outcomes of point of view (Chapter 5) and description (Chapter 3) ensure a focus on the observed data.

Identity triggers are not about the what (truth) or the other who (relationships). These behaviors that get in the way of accepting feedback are about the receiver: you! Something in the feedback caused you to look inward and now your confidence has been shaken.

4. View These Skills Not Just for Classroom Observation Feedback

Throughout the book, various references to protocols, or structured conversations, have been provided. It is no accident that Decatur emerged with the content of the High-Quality Feedback Innovation Configuration Map. They had been using protocols for years for their own development as leaders, especially as they started to learn about observation and feedback principles. As they carefully framed their feedback to each other, following the protocol parameters and guided by skilled facilitators, they experienced firsthand the power of using description, conditional language, point of view, and assumption-identification. These leaders already saw the value of interacting in these ways, and now it was time to apply that kind of learning more broadly to other areas, such as written classroom observation feedback.

Three examples provide relevant application across other school functions other than teacher evaluation. The first example poses the inadvertent gap leaders often create when asking teachers to do one thing but then the leaders do another.

Larry Ferlazzo (2015) cites Rick Wormeli in a blog post, adeptly painting the picture of what happens when we don't practice what we preach:

> *Here's What, So What, Now What* is one of the great formats for teachers to use when giving descriptive feedback to students: "Here's what I noticed about your work . . . ," "So this means you understand how to . . . and the differences between . . . ," and, "Now, let's create the next steps in your process . . ." Another effective format for descriptive feedback, *Point-and-Describe,* comes from Fay and Funk's *Love & Logic* books: "I noticed you had your notes on the left side of the double-entry journal so you

had quick access to that information as you worked the problems on the right side." Descriptive feedback in many assessment books consists of three parts: identifying the learning goal, determining where a student is operating in relation to that goal, and identifying what the teacher and student need to do in order to close the gap between the two.

In each of these techniques we focus on decisions students make and the outcomes of those decisions, not so much the quality of their work. This is much less threatening, and it allows students to internalize the feedback and use it, resulting in maturation and higher quality work: Instead of, "Nicely organized project," we observe, "I noticed you decided to control for salinity factors first in this project. Tell me more about that decision." There's no judgment here, as judgment slows reflection and learning. Observing what decisions were made and their impact on the intended course helps students retain autonomy: they can change decisions and achieve different results.

Of course, we want teachers to provide descriptive feedback to their students, so we train them on these techniques, then sit back and watch them fly.

Except they don't.

A few teachers give descriptive feedback an initial try, then run out of steam, returning to their lessons devoid of descriptive feedback. What went wrong? They were given the specific tools to use with students, and they clearly understood their value.

Most likely, the teachers weren't committed to descriptive feedback because they never experienced its positive benefits personally. Teachers are more inclined to provide descriptive feedback and other successful teaching practices to their students when they experience those same practices themselves. When teachers write reflectively and make better decisions as a result, they can't wait to help students write and reflect in class. When teachers are committed to a fit lifestyle, they are apt to include such thinking and activities in their work with students. When teachers feel the benefits of helpful and emotionally safe feedback from colleagues and administrators and they improve their teaching as a result, they are excited to offer those positive feedback experiences to students. And even better, they are empathetic with their students' experiences, knowing how to frame feedback in constructive ways students hear and use.

(Republished with permission of Rick Wormeli.)

This lack of congruence causes dissonance with teachers but also creates problems with other staff, too. The second example uses classroom observation experiences as a catalyst for other evaluations leaders are required to write. Principals and central office leaders often supervise other leaders, usually using a different evaluation process than what is used for teachers. Leadership evaluation processes often do not require an observation—in fact, I do not know of one that does. However, what if the same desired outcomes used for high-quality feedback for teachers were applied to leaders?

Upon being called up to the podium at the Board of Education meeting, eye contact was made: "Thank you for this opportunity to talk with you about the 1:1 project at our school."

The title slide of the presentation was immediately bypassed rather than read, and the second slide was displayed. Approximately two minutes were spent on slides 2 and 3. For both of these slides, the words on the slide were not directly read to the Board. Slide two had nine lines of text and three sentences were spoken to summarize.

Slide 4: "This is the most important part of our project thus far." A majority of the presentation—five minutes—was spent on this slide. A 90-second video, composed of teacher and student quips, was used. Each clip was audible and intelligible with the exception of the penultimate student. For that student, a line of text flashed on the bottom of the screen that indicated what she said. Each Board member smiled as they watched the video. The clip played immediately—the preparation to have it queued up was worth it.

After the last slide, deference was paid to the chair: "Thank you so much. How might you like to handle any questions?"

Each Board member spoke, but not each one had questions. For the member that asked three questions, responses were always three sentences or less. The question, "What will your technology choices be five years from now?" acknowledged something the school has not considered yet. Answer: "That is important for us to think about— thank you! We haven't discussed our plans five years in the future."

Even with the question and answer time included, the item stayed within the 20 minutes allotted on the agenda.

This central office supervisor wrote this during the presentation. Five minutes later, it was emailed to the principal.

The final example contextualizes how to build a culture of feedback in a large 2,000-student comprehensive high school. It has become very common to use protocols at Alpharetta High School in Georgia. Significant resources have been secured for professional development in the School Reform Initiative critical friendship. Newly hired staff are immersed in structured processes even before they begin their official orientation.

The days at the end of the school, post-planning, are characterized by sessions held to receive feedback on changes considered for the next school year. One block of time in May, 2015, looked like the following:

- Honor Code Policy (Frank Fortunato), Room 2218
- RISE/Recovery policy and practice (Tina Johnson), Room 2213
- Senior Exemptions (Rebecca Perkins), Room 2224
- Dress Code (Laurie Veillon), Room 2210
- Anchor Time (Pollye Bostick), Room 2317
- Protecting instructional time with a 10/10 rule (Charles Chester), Room 4223

Certain staff members were identified to "hold" the issue for the school and carefully considered the outcomes of the session in order to choose a process or protocol that would help get them there. As a school beginning to use a shared governance model, students, parents, and staff members were all invited to attend.

The leadership team met two days later to consider the feedback gathered in these sessions. Staff members used a common template to prepare for this time:

1. Topic
2. Change Recommended (if any)
3. *Working Assumptions*
4. Impact of Change
5. Rationale

Note the italicized text: lifting up and examining assumptions is now part of the fabric of how adults work together at Alpharetta. It would be inconsistent for their written feedback about classroom observations to not have the same level of thoughtfulness as the rest of their work.

Shifts

Perhaps it is helpful to think about the conceptual shifts you might make as you employ these desired outcomes of description, conditional language, consistent point of view, explicit assumptions, and attention to co-teaching models and equity.

From Evaluator to Data Collector

Remember DIE? Data collectors describe. Think of a census worker coming to your home because you neglected to fill out the decennial survey: they are asking for description—it may feel invasive, but *the worker* is not interpreting the results. His job is to collect.

After spending 100% of your observation energy in classrooms collecting, feel free to add interpretation and evaluation to create a final written product that is still at least 80% description.

From Data Collected About Them *to* for Them

Throughout this book, I consistently use this phrase: "the reader, the teacher." Just like we teach young writers, our students, that audience matters, then audience should matter for us, too. When we believe that the descriptive data we collect, then interpret, is *for* our colleagues' growth and their opportunity to autosupervise, it changes our stance.

From Data Collected to Them *to* for Them

Similar to the last shift, a significant majority of teachers have not experienced teacher evaluation processes that have been *for them;* rather, it has been done *to them.* Certainly using the desired outcomes described in this book will change that perspective, but changing the how is only one facet of the change. The frequency needs to change as well.

This is not to pose that simply raising the frequency of observations will make a positive difference. The state of Georgia moved from a primarily once/year observation process to six times/year. Simply changing the frequency and now using a four-point rubric instead of a two-point scale did not automatically create meaningful observation practices. In fact, in many places it simply took a marginal practice and increased it six-fold.

When the desired outcomes described in this book are consistently practiced and used, there is more time for additional observations. Well-intentioned observers should not be spending precious weekend hours trying to find "just the right" language. Building the discipline to "live in description" creates the conditions for teachers to use these written narratives as professional development, not limited to evaluation. And we know that when teachers experience something meaningful, they crave it!

From Positive/Negative to Productive

Consider the last time you debated whether you should say something because of how it may be received. Where in DIE where you? Probably evaluation, as you were concerned how the person might judge either the content or the person delivering the content—you!

Start reframing those moments in this way: *Will this feedback be productive?* Focusing on positive or negative reactions often forces us to rethink the content. The reframed question often keeps the content steady while prompting the feedback giver to contemplate what conditions will be needed in order for the reader, the teacher, to accept and consider the feedback.

Closing

Language matters. Chapters 3–8 each started with this maxim, and now we use it to close. Yes, the words we use definitely matter, but just changing the words is not enough. The aforementioned shifts are not simply about using different words. If that were the case, this book would simply be a reservoir of phrases and sentences that "magically" create effective observation narratives. Well-meaning leaders would lift the phrases, utilize copy and paste, and smile, believing they have one less skill to demonstrate for their informal professional growth plan.

Narratives that would all look the same do not require *crafting*. My wife loves to attend craft fairs. I am consistently amazed not only at the products people have produced, but at the uniqueness of each item.

As crafters craft, they are not reproducing widgets; rather, their pieces have differences, and the crafters are unapologetic about that fact. We as educational leaders do not wish for teachers to treat each child equally, for if we do, we will not have equitable outcomes. Similarly, our classroom observation feedback need not be equal for each teacher; instead, we equitably work for each teacher's development. Each teacher deserves the opportunity to become consciously competent. This book has provided the desired outcomes you can work toward and the criteria by which to assess your work. Perhaps you are now working in the light, having illuminated a dark place in your leadership.

Language matters. Our shifting and changing language is more emblematic of our purpose—which may be a new purpose or a more clearly defined one: *creating the conditions where more teachers can autosupervise*. Consistently demonstrating the desired outcomes on the High-Quality Feedback Innovation Configuration Map gives us a significant head start toward building a culture of feedback by crafting the feedback teachers need and deserve. Craft away.

Try It Yourself

1. As a school or a district, try using the High-Quality Feedback Innovation Configuration Map, setting your own acceptable variations denoted by gray boxes. For your first year, what will be acceptable as you create space for you and your faculty to learn what it takes to craft high-quality feedback?

2. Consider Principal Thomas's example: videotaping yourself teaching a lesson and asking faculty to craft high-quality feedback that meet the same purposes as the desired outcomes on the High-Quality Feedback Innovation Configuration Map.

3. What other parts of your leadership practice might already be conceptually aligned to these skills and desired outcomes? It might be possible align your ever-developing written observation skills to other current practices.

4. Ask others to collect data for you in your practice: a leadership team meeting, a faculty gathering, a parent conference. Plan how to share your learning with your faculty, explicitly connecting to the feedback you craft for them.

5. Apply the High-Quality Feedback Innovation Configuration Map to one of the five written narratives in the appendix. Consider annotating the text like a student involved in a close reading strategy. After reading it several times, use the map to assess its quality.

Reference List

Arneson, S. (2015). Improving teaching one conversation at a time. *Educational Leadership, 72*(7), 32–36.

Bambrick-Santoyo, P. (2012). *Leverage leadership.* San Francisco, CA: Jossey-Bass.

Drago-Severson, E., & Blum-DeStefano, J. (2014). Tell me so I can hear: A developmental approach to feedback and collaboration. *Journal of Staff Development, 35*(6), 16–22.

Ferlazzo, L. (2015). *The kind of professional development we need.* Retrieved from http://blogs.edweek.org/teachers/classroom_qa_with_larry_ferlazzo/2015/05/response_the_kind_of_professional_development_we_need.html?cmp=ENL-EU-NEWS2-RM.

Marshall, K. (2009). *Rethinking teacher supervision and evaluation: How to work smart, build collaboration, and close the achievement gap.* San Francisco, CA: Jossey-Bass.

Stone, D., & Heen, S. (2014). *Thanks for the feedback: The art and science of receiving feedback well.* New York, NY: Random House.

Van Soelen, T.M. (2003). *If Polly had been there: An uncommon journey toward teacher development and induction* (Unpublished doctoral dissertation). University of Georgia, Athens, GA.

Appendix

Narrative #1, High School Grades

Students were in groups completing a lab about soil permeability. Students moved around the room at different times, quite clear where to access materials.

Students needed to pace themselves as a six-day lab with 10 activities. Two students in the middle of the room were talking about unrelated content for seven minutes and then moved to assist others, offering feedback to other groups about their lab setup.

More than three students were working on assignments from other classes (e.g., calculus).

The fourth lab from the Carolina Biological Supply Company includes three written required responses at various Depth of Knowledge (DOK) levels: one at DOK 1, one at DOK 2, one at DOK 3.

When asked about what she was learning, a student offered the topic of soil permeability and today's findings. When asked, *"So, why does this matter?"* With a three-second pause and a giggle, she offered the following: *"I guess if I was planting something, I would know what kind of soil to use."* We are wondering if this answer is at the cognitive level you would hope for at this stage of their learning and the experiment.

The board did not include objectives, essential questions, or standards.

Students had check-ins regarding their progress on the tasks. A tension might exist in how much support to provide students as they develop the independence needed for college courses. However, we are curious if our responsibility here is different, and we would include more frequent check-ins on their understanding of the learning outcomes.

Narrative #2, Upper Elementary Grades

Essential questions were posted: *"How did the revolution fighting begin? How did TJ use his words in the DI?"* Consider how these questions can be crafted in deeper, more thoughtful ways.

Content knowledge is demonstrated, specifically when one student in particular added numerous details. The details were affirmed or refuted.

Students sat in chairs listening to a story about the Revolutionary War. Four questions were asked; male voices answered.

Instruction stopped both times an interruption occurred: a young lady coming in with tissue and a young man with a pass. Consider how you might be able to keep thinking and talking while people come in and out of the classroom.

One student had a cell phone out during class. At some point during the observation, every student did write something down.

Assumptions are made about what students retain or understand when they copy notes. Consider other ways that students could be engaged, particularly when the content of the day is chronologically taught. Perhaps there could be an overarching, deeper question posed at the beginning of the period (e.g., Essential Question) that the students wouldn't be able to answer until the full story is told.

Narrative #3, Middle School Grades

Student work was posted on one wall. A "While you were out" bulletin board was used with papers coming out of several folders. Seventeen commercially created posters are on the wall.

Nineteen students were working on an acrostic, and then transitioned to annotating a text. It is unclear if students were fully knowledgeable of this intent of the acrostic. When asked about the annotating, students said:

- *"Annotating helps me make real-world connections."*
- *"Annotating helps it make sense to me."*

Two standards were posted as well as the EQ: *"How do we read for meaning in an informational text?"*

One student had trouble finding his annotation sheet. One way to keep track of these sheets is to keep another copy in the room, taped to individual desks. There are 14 items on the Annotated Text support. It may be informative for you to do some informal tracking of which annotations they use the most—it may be that some are more meaningful than others.

At the beginning of the observation, initial directions were given regarding the acrostic and responding to the quote. One group of students was talking during this direction-giving.

At one point during the class period, all talking ceased as students were reading and preparing to annotate.

Eight times while students were working, they were interrupted with additional directions or redirections.

When needing redirection, the phrase *"Guys, focus"* was used multiple times.

The group size was either two or six. It is unclear about the intentionality of these groups. When asked about their groups, a student mentioned that they have been in these groups all year and are not sure why. Consider how equitable students' voices will be in each group with a size of six. Perhaps 4–5 students in each group would be possible using a different desk arrangement.

Work was organized around three areas:

- Preparing to read
- Before reading
- After reading

The task required students to work at high levels. For instance, *"Explain why you believe what you believe."*

Every student is reading the same text and using the same set of annotation marks. This text is at a 6.1 grade level according to https://readability-score.com/.

Narrative #4, High School Grades

It is unclear what standards were being addressed in this lesson as lesson plans were not provided in hard copy, nor were they present in Eduphoria.

Instructional Strategies

Twenty-six students were working in various groups/partnerships around the room.

One student was working on math homework. When asked, students said they were either working on the following:

- Becoming a commentator for a soccer game
- We watched a movie in Spanish and now we are making a script like we are interviewing each other as characters from the movie.

It is unclear if the difficulty of the assignment is the same for each student in the room or if choice was present.

Students were using devices for various purposes: looking up Spanish vocabulary and verb conjugations, reviewing soccer video footage, or texting other students. Sometimes students would not use their electronic or print resources. They would ask aloud how to spell certain words or what certain words meant. They were always provided the answer.

In listening in as students worked together, 90–95% of student talk connected to the assignment. Approximately 70% was spoken in English. We are curious what the target percentage might be for the target language in this Spanish III class.

Five minutes of this 10-minute observation was spent asking students (in English) if they had submitted or re-submitted assignments. *"I'll give you extra points for that."*

When one partnership received direct feedback on their work, students were asked what they were really trying to say:

S: *[response]*
T: *"I just don't know how to word this. I'm not sure why it sounds weird to me."*
S: *[response]*
T: *"Take yourself out of the past tense and put yourself in the present tense."*

After multiple attempts and prompts, the answer was given to the students.

Positive Learning Environment

Students moved around the room, moving desks and chairs to accommodate themselves. Posters and some student work were present on the walls.

Narrative #5, Primary Grades

There are 20 students sitting on the carpet looking at the poem, "Little Boy Blue," on a colored chart. This nursery rhyme is being used to teach rhyming. The student teacher was sitting on a chair watching instruction.

Sample responses to students:

- *"We are listening for something that rhymes with horn."*
- *"What do you think, E?"*
- When students spoke out loud without being called on: *"It's Chloe's turn, let's listen to Chloe."*

Two moments of a formative strategy:

1. *"If you think these two words rhyme, put both hands on your head."*
   All students but one put their hands on their head.
   "M, why are both hands on top of your head?" Students saw a model of both hands on an adult head.
2. *"If you think that X rhymes with Y, put your pinky on your nose."*
   Students saw a model of a pinky on a nose.
   "Why do you have your pinky on your nose? . . . because my pinky is on my nose, so you did it too?"

Young children clearly model physical moments by an adult. If this formative strategy is continued, consider just using words to identify the movement rather than also modeling it. Then it clearly can offer formative data for consideration.

One attribute of rhyming words was offered: *"Rhyming words are different at the beginning."* It is unclear whether this "difference" was about the sound or the actual letter.

A student added another attribute: *"Both words have the same sound at the end."*

"M, we are finding something that rhymes with sheep."

"M, eyes on poem."

It seems the important learning for students was about hearing the rhyme, not seeing it in print. Considering the size of the font on the colored chart, for students that cannot see the text, simply listening for the rhyme meets that objective. If it would be important for students to see the text, some ways to manage that would be to enlarge the print, to break into two groups with two copies of the chart, or to project the text.

"Find a rhyme, what's a rhyme?"

The last two lines of the poem were then read.

A second attribute is given near the end of the observation: *"Rhyming words are the same at the end."*

It may be helpful to quickly summarize the two attributes of this mini-lesson before moving on to something else:

1. Rhyming words are different at the beginning. (Consider whether this will be about the sound or the actual letter.)

2. Rhyming words are the same at the end. (same thought)